Our churches are packed with peop... actually do anything he said! This book will make you laugh and cry. It will make you look at things in a fresh new way. And it will definitely make you uncomfortable. Which might be a good thing because ultimately Dan calls us to live, love, and lead like the Jesus we claim to follow.

— RAY JOHNSTON, AUTHOR OF THE HOPE QUOTIENT AND FOUNDING AND LEAD PASTOR AT BAYSIDE CHURCH, ROSEVILLE, CALIFORNIA

Most Christian books are about our most important vertical relationship— us and God—but this book explores what those books don't: the horizontal relationship we are called to as human beings—the relationships we must have with one another. Indeed, this is a lost art that Dan recovers and teaches us about with heart and logic at every turn. I highly recommend it!

— MARK CLARK, AUTHOR OF THE PROBLEM OF GOD AND LEAD PASTOR AT VILLAGE CHURCH, SURREY, BRITISH COLUMBIA, CANADA

I still recall the first time Dan came into my office. I couldn't understand why he was so persistent in us meeting. I wondered, what did he want? It didn't take long before I found out...a relationship with me, a stranger whom he only knew by name! He began with wanting to hear my story. I wanted to hand him a copy of my book *Five Years to Life* but decided against it. I then asked him to tell me his story. I don't recall much of it because I never got beyond the story of his father and how he crossed cultural barriers and built relationships lasting over thirty-plus years with individuals that started out as strangers.

This let me know what was "in" Dan. By the time he was done telling me that story I knew we would be brothers. We have had many meetings since that initial one. We have laughed, cried, and ate a lot together...maybe too much! Dan has the gift of risk-taking in seeking out and building relationships. As he writes in this book, step one in building relationships is noticing someone, the last step if you get that far is you become family. If you want a quick fix to relationships, don't read this book. But, if you want to learn how to build life-long, meaningful friendships, then this book might be for you.

I would recommend this book not because of Dan's deep research into the subject, but because the subject matter is deeply in him. Dan has made his life's journey living out *The Lost Art of Relationship*.

— DR. SAM HUDDLESTON, ASSISTANT SUPERINTENDENT ASSEMBLIES OF GOD, NORTHERN CALIFORNIA DISTRICT, AND AUTHOR OF *FIVE YEARS TO LIFE*

The Lost Art of Relationship is a fun and fascinating read that reveals stunning insights for loving people and cultivating relationships. It's easy to focus all of our Christian walk on developing relationship with God to the point that we forget to apply God's command in loving others. Loving others is not easy, and sadly, many Christians don't do it well. Dan beautifully illuminates our kingdom mandate while providing brilliant insights, practical steps, engaging stories, and revelations at every turn. Particularly revelatory are the pitfalls and mistakes so many of us make that cost us vibrant and healthy relationships. If you want to fulfill the commandment of loving others (and do it well), this book is must-read.

— ERIC KNOPF, CO-FOUNDER OF WEBCONNEX LLC AND FOUNDER OF EPIC LIFE

What is refreshing about this book is that it not only contains incredible insight and wisdom, but it authentically represents Dan Chrystal. His transparency will undoubtedly touch your heart. I met Dan several years ago at our large church where I served as a pastor. I quickly observed that Dan is one of the most skillful people I have ever met at intentionally developing deep and healthy friendships. Dan is authentic and caring and it shows in the vast number of people who have the blessing of knowing him and their deep affection for him. This book contains the thoughtful wisdom Dan applies to his relationships. I highly and enthusiastically recommend this book as I know anyone who reads and applies it will walk away a better friend, spouse, worker, and person.

— DAN HOUK, PASTOR OF SHADOW MOUNTAIN SOUTH BAY CAMPUS, SAN DIEGO, CALIFORNIA

I heard and, most importantly, have watched Dan Chrystal communicate and live out these principles almost a decade ago. I am so thrilled that he has taken the leap to make these timeless and practical truths available to a larger audience. Not only are you going to enjoy this book, I have a strong hunch that you will never forget it and recommend it to others!

— GAVIN BROWN, SENIOR PASTOR OF LIFEHOUSE CHURCH, BELTSVILLE, MARYLAND, WWW.MYLIFEHOUSE.CHURCH

The Lost Art of Relationship is like a road map to finding, building, and treasuring friendships. In spite of all of the "friends" we may have through social media, never before have people seemed so adrift of meaningful, face-to-face relationships. Dan's book provides practical "how-to" advice on finding, building, and valuing close friendships. If you are someone who longs for deeper connections, then Dan's book was written for you!

— CHRIS BUENO, CHIEF EXECUTIVE OFFICER OF OCEAN AVENUE ENTERTAINMENT

Dan and I have lived out the contents of this book through our friendship. I believe Dan's heart for relationships is one of the keys to releasing the kingdom of heaven on earth. My prayer is that everyone who reads this book will be inspired by Dan to become an artist in the golden rule and see God's heart in action.

— DAVE DREVER, FOUNDER AND CHIEF EXECUTIVE OFFICER AT FREELY

Dan Chrystal has written a must-read for anyone considering leading others. His professional personal experiences and knowledge of people make this book a must-read for anyone desiring to build healthy teams and relationships.

— HEIDI HENSLEY, CHILDREN'S PASTOR AT SHADOW MOUNTAIN CHURCH, SAN DIEGO, CALIFORNIA

The Lost Art of Relationship

A Journey to Find the Lost Commandment

DAN CHRYSTAL

THE SOPHOS GROUP

The Lost Art of Relationship: A Journey to Find the Lost Commandment
Copyright © 2018 by Dan Chrystal

Published by The Sophos Group, Lincoln, CA 95648. All Rights Reserved. For more information about this book and the author, email TheSophosGroup@gmail.com.

Copyedited by:
Jennifer Edwards
jedwardsediting.net

Book design by:
Linné Garrett
829 DESIGN
829Design.com

Cover design by:
Susie Aguirre

Book cover photo by Arthur Poulin on Unsplash.com

Print book ISBN: 978-1-7327564-0-3
E-book ISBN: 978-1-7327564-1-0
Audio book ISBN: 978-1-7327564-2-7

Library of Congress Cataloging Number: 2018910544

Printed in the United States of America.

✤ Dedications ✤

This project is dedicated to the following people in my life:

MY MOM.
You passed from this life way too soon.
Your example of how to connect with others and serve them
in love has shaped who I am today. I will always love and
remember you and promise to carry on your legacy
for as long as I live.

PASTOR VICTOR COETZEE.
You taught me more in one year of ministry than I learned in
four years of education. I am so grateful I was placed under your leadership
when I first graduated college. You believed in me, mentored and taught me,
and showed me by your example what it means to
love your neighbor as yourself.

TO ALL THOSE WHO LIVED WHAT JESUS COMMANDED—
*to love God with all your heart, all your soul, and all your mind,
and love your neighbor as yourself.* Your life was not lived in vain
but has left a mark on so many more than
you could ever imagine.

✤ Contents ✤

⚜ Foreword ⚜

I WANT TO START THIS FOREWORD WITH A QUESTION...*ARE YOU HAPPY?*

There's an academic journal called *The Journal of Happiness Studies,* and they're trying to use the tools of research to figure out what it is that makes human life flourish and what produces joy. I thought this was quite interesting. When they looked at what distinguishes more happy people from less happy people, they found that there is one factor, one difference that consistently separates those two groups. What is it? I'll bet you're curious.

It's not income. It's not how much money you have. It's not health. It's not what kind of shape your body is in. It's not security. It's not attractiveness. It's not IQ. It's not career success. What distinguishes consistently happier people from less happy people is the presence of rich, deep, joy-producing, life-changing, meaningful relationships with other human beings.

A guy named Robert Putnam wrote a book in this last decade called Bowling Alone. It's maybe the most influential kind of analysis of social wellbeing in the last ten years (until this book!). This is one of the things he wrote,

> *"The single most common finding from a half-century's research
> on life satisfaction not only from the US but around the world,
> is that happiness is best predicted by the breadth and depth of
> one's social connections."*

In other words, the best predictor of whether or not you will live with joy and contentment is your relationships. In our world, you will see a half million media messages telling you that happiness is just one purchase away. Why do you think they call it a Happy Meal? In *The Lost Art of Relationship,* Dan explains that happiness is not *what*—it's *Who!*

Of course, that's not news to God because God made us that way. The Bible said this a long time ago. God created human beings, and then *"The Lord God said, 'It is not good for man to be alone.'"* (Gen. 2:18)

The destructive aspects of isolation are unbelievably powerful. Disconnected people are more emotionally isolated and are prone to depression, anxiety, loneliness, low self-esteem, substance abuse, sexual addiction, and difficulties with eating and sleeping—all because it is not good to be alone...that's disconnection physically and emotionally. It takes a huge toll.

Listen, this is how strong this is. People who have bad health habits, like cigarette smoking, overeating, elevated blood pressure, and physical inactivity but are connected, *live longer* than people who have great health habits but are disconnected and isolated.

The poster boy for this might be Winston Churchill. Churchill had deep connections. He had a wonderful marriage, was connected to his family, his friends, his nation, and his work. His health habits were terrible. His diet was awful. He smoked cigars all the time. He drank too much, had weird sleep habits, was completely sedentary, but he lived to be the ripe old age of ninety! Somebody questioned him one time, *"Winston, do you ever exercise?"* This was his response, *"The only exercise I get is serving as a pallbearer for my friends who died while they were exercising."* This could be the power of connection.

This is the *best* practical book on building relationships that I have read this year! And just in time. Why? Because today most people have hundreds of *online* friends—but no *real-life* relationships. I have talked to hundreds of people who tell me, *"I can't find friends."* That's why I tell them great friendships are never "found"—they are "built." This book will give you all the tools you need to start building!

— PASTOR RAY JOHNSTON
Author of *The Hope Quotient*
Founding Pastor of Bayside Church
Granite Bay, California

September 2018

✤ Acknowledgments ✤

✤

This book did not happen without relationships. There have been so many people in my life that have played a role in teaching me about how to love your neighbor as yourself.

The most important relationship in my life is with God. Jesus did so much to show how much He loved me. I only want to honor Him in everything I say and do, loving Him with all my mind, all my strength, and all my heart.

After God, the most important person in my life is the amazing woman I get to spend my life with, my wife, Tania. She has been the greatest champion, support, love, partner, and spouse a man could ever ask for. I love you, Tania! Thank you so much for cheering me on!

I would like to thank both of my daughters, Margaux and Miriam. Thank you for your love, your passion, and your lives. You both have always encouraged me to lean into my passions and desires for ministry. I only want to be the best example of a father to you.

My dad has been one of the best examples of a man who lives what he believes, acts on what he teaches, and honors God and others. Thank you, Dad, for believing in me and saying the words over and over, "You can do whatever you set your mind to. Your mom and I love you and only want you to do your best at what you choose to do." I love you, dad!

Thank you, Ken and Tara Nelson, for giving me your daughter, Tania, in marriage. This was the single greatest gift you could have ever given. Your encouragement and prayers have been incredible.

To my best friend in college, Brian Coscia, thank you for the long talks, brotherly love, prayers, and always just picking up where we left off when we talk. I love you like a brother and only wish that our life's journey would have been way closer than across the country.

Thank you, Dr. Greg Miller, for your mentorship during the six-month period that shaped my ministry, decisions, and relationships for the rest of my life!

To my ever-questioning, always-loving friend, Brian Griswold, thank you for being the example of not being afraid to go for it! Your quest for the answers to questions has inspired me to always dig deeper in relationship.

To Gavin Brown, thank you, my friend, for being authentic, for loving life and laughter, for helping me see the funny in most everything, for praying with me, and encouraging me with your life. So glad we shared so many moments that will be forever in my memory.

Thank you, Steve Preston, for believing in me, being available to teach me, mentor me, and encourage me even in some of the darkest moments. You taught me so much about relationships, just by being a friend—and never afraid to hold me accountable!

To our incredible friends, Dan and Teresa Houk. There are not many relationships one will have in life where you can share ANYTHING and never feel like you shouldn't. You both are that for Tania and I. Thank you for giving us your love, care, prayers, and friendship, and for the encouragement to FINISH this book and get it into as many hands as possible! We love you so much!

To our wonderful friends, John and Laura Volinsky. It is so great to have people in life that like to have fun but are there for you when it counts. John, thank you for giving me a chance in ministry and for being a champion for me. You both are prayer warriors, and we love you!

For my good friend Dr. Sam Huddleston. Your example in leadership and how to be in relationship with others has been more than a blessing in my life. Being able just to call or text and say what is on my mind is a breath of fresh air. I am so grateful for your friendship and for how God has connected us.

Thank you, Rick Bloom, for guiding me to renew my credentials when I moved from Santa Maria to Los Angeles. You were a pivotal part of my continuing in the ministry and having the tools necessary to move forward!

To my friends Joe Taybron, Charlie Harrison, and Scott Lewis. The endless amount of connections because of my friendships with you are still becoming known! Thank you for including me in your circles of influence!

To my editor, Jennifer Edwards. Thank you for your incredible expertise and believing in this project to take the time to organize it, edit it, and make it way better and understandable! This book cannot be what it is without your influence!

Thank you, Susie Aguirre, for putting your fingerprint of design on the cover and for taking the time to help capture what the *Lost Art of Relationship* is all about—authentic relationships with others in awe of God, sharing in connection the way God intended.

Thank you, Chris Bueno and Dave Drever, for your friendship, coffee times, investing in prayer for my family and me, and for allowing me into your lives. I cannot wait to see what is still yet to come because of our relationships!

Thank you, Eric Unterberger, for taking on the promotional challenge of this project! So many more people will come to understand how to love their neighbor as themselves because of your design expertise, relentless desire to get the message of Christ out, and simply to help people get an idea from concept to reality!

What can I say about Eric Knopf? This guy has the drive to keep moving forward like a freight train in business, ministry, and life! He loves God, loves his family, and wants to use what God has provided him to elevate others and give them a platform for their ideas. You are an example to me, and I will be forever grateful for your belief in me and in this project. I am stoked to see how our friendship will have a lasting influence on as many lives as we can impact!

To the fantastic group of people that read this book when it was first written, and you offered your feedback, edits, changes, time, and prayers—thank you so much! Your time and critical feedback were more valuable than you may ever know! This focus group included the following beautiful souls...Karen Kiyoko Bregar, Captain Molly Lawlor, Hannah Montez, Mariann Eitzman, Zach Dutra, Paul Bryers, and Chris Bueno. We made it to the finish line!

Thank you to Brené Brown for your research, your TED Talk, and incredible insights into vulnerability and relationship! I have not met you, but it would be phenomenal to get you, Bono from U2, and Elon Musk around a dinner table so we could exchange life stories!

Thank you to every relational connection I have ever had, have, and will have wherever I get to do life! There are still so many people I am excited to meet! If you are reading this, email me at thesophosgroup@gmail.com and introduce yourself! Maybe one day our paths will cross.

Finally, I want to thank from the bottom of my heart, Roger Flessing. It was on a summer day three years ago where you said something that brought this project into reality. I had started and never finished at least fifteen books because I could not decide what I should write about. You asked if I had stories. I said, "yes." You said, "Just start writing your stories, and after about four or five of them, you will know exactly what you are supposed to write about." Four or five stories later, the *Lost Art of Relationship* was born. Thank you for your wisdom and friendship.

✢ Introduction ✢

THE BEGINNING

I had my first "job" when I was twelve years old. I remember going to church one Sunday, and my father introduced me to a man named John Kafka. He held out his hand to shake mine, and as a twelve-year-old, I simply took his hand, but he shook mine with a death grip. He said to me, "Danny, it is nice to meet you. May I tell you something that will help you with your future?" I said, "Yes, sir." He replied, "Whenever you shake someone's hand, show confidence. You squeeze that person's hand, so they know you are confident. A good, firm handshake says a lot about who you are to others." I will never forget that first lesson he gave me.

My father had always taught me to show respect for others, not to lie, and to work hard. I still think my dad talked to John Kafka beforehand and asked him to become a mentor to me at the tender age of twelve. John Kafka was the president of Pollock Johnny's, a polish sausage restaurant chain based in Baltimore, and he owned a house in a more expensive neighborhood. He was a wealthy man who had worked hard to get to where he was, yet he still wore clothes from the thrift store. He gave me a job at his house making twenty-eight dollars every Saturday to weed the rock garden behind his house and on the hill behind the in-ground pool. It was a tough job, but it strengthened my hands and arm muscles, so I didn't have to work so hard to give a firm handshake. My dad dropped me off before he went to work and picked me up nine hours later.

I would not realize it until later, but John Kafka taught me so much about the importance of relationship. I learned that every relationship needs to be mutual; most of the time, we need to work hard at maintaining healthy relationships; and some of the most beneficial relationships can happen through tragic circumstances.

I will never forget the night. It was a Thursday night, and I had just finished taking a shower. My dad knocked on the bathroom door and asked if he could come in. I asked him to tell me through the door since I wasn't decent. He said to me that John Kafka had just died that day. He was playing racquetball and fell dead in the middle of a game. I took the news pretty hard. I sank to the floor leaning on the door of the bathroom and cried.

Not only was he the first person to give me a job, but he was the first person (other than my father, who I consider my hero) to teach me valuable lessons about hard work, discipline, and the importance of relationship. I did not know it then, but the lessons on relationship would deepen in the coming year.

John's wife, Marge Kafka, asked me to continue coming and helping around the outside of the house. I weeded the rock garden and all around their flower beds. It was a lot of territory to cover. I was now thirteen, making fifty dollars every Saturday.

An unexpected thing happened while I worked there for Marge. She invited me in to have lunch, and we spent two to three hours every Saturday just talking and keeping each other company. She had become very lonely with her kids out of the house and her husband gone. I always worried that I wasn't getting the work completed, but she reassured me that her money was being well spent.

What I discovered later was that she desired relationship and companionship, conversation, and a feeling of belonging. She found it in a thirteen-year-old teenager. During a time when a teenager's life typically becomes more about them than others, I was learning the importance of time well-spent with someone who needed connection. I'm convinced she saw me as her adopted grandson. She even let me swim in her pool on the hot Saturdays after I got done working until my dad came to pick me up. I only worked for Marge another eighteen months until I was old enough to get a job in a bookstore closer to home.

I learned many valuable lessons, such as the significance of putting others first, that merely being there for someone matters, the importance of a firm handshake, the value of hard work, and the necessity of seeing value in others. These formed the basis of almost thirty years and counting of learning about relationships that continues today and will until my life is over. I am forever grateful to the Kafkas for teaching me so much.

THE WONDER YEARS

Have you ever seen the show *The Wonder Years?* I loved that show.

During some of my teenage years, I felt a lot like Kevin Arnold. It was an age of discovery, identity, and development. I sometimes "wonder" how I made it out of that part of my life! That may be why they named the show that name. And yes, it always helps to have a brother who is older and in the same high school, at least for a year.

I was in ninth grade. Somehow, I had made a name for myself, but at first, it was through my brother. I had gone from someone who was ridiculed (don't get me wrong, I did have friends but I was very insecure), had body parts all growing at different rates, and was what some would call nerdy, to someone who was accepted, finally having hands and feet that matched the rest of my body…and, well, still nerdy.

My brother was in the twelfth grade and had already made friends. I became known as "the little brother." I had also joined the Mock Trial club and became a mock-lawyer. That year our team went all the way to the state regionals in Annapolis, Maryland, though we lost in the semi-finals. But, I managed to obtain the name "Mad-Dog Dan" for ripping a piece of evidence out of the hand of the other team's witness.

Also, that year, I started attending a youth group at a church called Trinity. They had a guest speaker come who was to visit six high schools. His name is Dave Roever, a Vietnam Veteran with a phenomenal story of triumph over tragedy that took place in his life. (You can find out more information about him at www.daveroever.org.)

After watching a video of his story in a high school auditorium, I was determined to make sure that my high school would be one of the six schools chosen. (This is where I learned the importance of networking and overcoming fears and insecurities for the sake of relationship and a higher purpose.)

The thoughts and fears that went through my mind were, "Why would the church youth leadership pick my school?" "You don't know anyone," "You're not important enough," and "They will look right past you." Fears can be crippling when trying to accomplish something. They can also be crippling when trying to build relationships with others.

The trouble with these insecurities and fears?

It turns out, no one else knows you are feeling them. It is like being trapped inside your mind and feeling as if no one can hear the inner screams of inadequacy. Thankfully, I had parents and friends who were very encouraging. I never heard from them, "You cannot do this." In fact, the opposite was true. My parents and friends continued to encourage me with words such as, "You can do anything you set your mind to."

I wonder what would have happened if I had not had people in my life that took the time to share encouragement, words of confidence and affirmation, and allowed me the freedom to "go for it." Even with those words, I struggled with assertiveness. However, pushing through those negative feelings allowed me the opportunity to bring the school a fantastic assembly—the first assembly in the school's history where the entire student body was allowed to attend.

That accomplishment set a precedent for my high school career. It opened doors of relationship with my teachers and other students, and although I still struggled with feelings of inadequacy, I had friends around me that spoke inspiration, support, and perseverance into my life.

These events taught me the value of being an encourager in relationships with others. It's never fun to be a part of a relationship where there is *little to no mutual* encouragement. Relationships work best when there is a healthy amount of support on both sides.

On that note, I encourage you to take the opportunity to be the *encourager* instead of the critic in one (or many) of your relationships: your spouse, your child, a friend going through a difficult moment in time, a co-worker, or even to someone you do not know, like a cashier, waiter or waitress, or others.

Encouragement is one of the most significant characteristics in the art of relationship. It can mean the difference in someone accomplishing something of value in their lives—encouragement can bring courage to someone who needs it.

A CHALLENGE FOR YOU

As you read this book, keep in mind the idea of intentionality in relationships. Think about how you are strategically placed to influence and impact those around you wherever you go. In Scripture, God has given us an imperative to love others as we love ourselves. Ask God to give you clarity in your current relationships and purpose in each connection you make going forward in your life. You are here for a reason, and healthy relationships is a big part of it.

There are three parts to this book. I will spend some time going over *Foundations of Relationship.* In part one, I will focus on what we need to form a stable base for any relationship in our lives. When you think of relationship, keep in mind this encompasses all types of relationships—family, friendships, work, marriage, children, church, school, and any person-to-person connection, including those we see at the grocery store, bank, coffee shops, and other places we frequent. I answer the questions: What are the foundations of relationship? Why do we rely so heavily on first impressions? What does it mean to have a servant's heart? What is the purpose of relationship? What does it mean to be a friend? How do we transcend differences and build unity with others, especially those not like us?

Part two, *Overcoming Obstacles in Relationship,* answers questions such as: What holds us back from making connections with others and deepening relationships? How does jealousy play a negative role in my life with others? Are we supposed to disconnect in relationship with others? Aren't we supposed to do our best to get along with everyone? How do you disengage from unhealthy relationships?

Finally, in part three, I will build on the foundations of relationship and discover the *Building Blocks of Relationship*. I will tackle topics like trust, love, honesty, influence, hope, humility, and how to build relationships by asking the right questions and taking on an attitude to be ever-learning about others, especially those closest to us.

My challenge to you is to set aside all that you know about relationship. Keep an open mind as we work through the issues we face in our relationships with each other. I also challenge you to think of yourself first—in sober judgment. It can be very easy to think of those in our lives who "really need to read this." However, just as the second most important thing to God is loving our neighbors as ourselves, we need to start with our own lives, beliefs, perspectives, pre-conceived notions, and growth points.

Once we can process where we are in our own thinking, how we act, talk, live, and treat others, we can then reach out and be the example to others. Once we begin to live out loving our neighbors as ourselves, our actions will be the influence. We have all heard that our actions speak louder than our words.

The challenge, in the end, is to live out the principles of this book. We can do that by learning from those around us on how to love our neighbor as ourselves.

Accept the challenge. Let's do this.

PART ONE

Foundations
of Relationship

I

The Art of Discovery

"Love your neighbor as yourself."
~ Jesus, Matthew 22:39

July 12, 1973, was an unusually windy and mild day in Baltimore, Maryland. In a month where the highest temperatures should be recorded, it was only seventy degrees Fahrenheit that day.

At 12:04 p.m., the cry of a baby boy filled the room. Mom had labored for hours and was exhausted. The first breaths were taken, and the earth welcomed another little human to its ranks. He was given a birth certificate, a social security number, and sent home with his family—mom, dad, and a brother, who was three years older than him.

He didn't have any choice about who his parents or siblings would be, nor what other children would be placed around him. When he was younger, he had to make friends with the kids in his neighborhood, plus those of his parents' friends and the church where his parents attended.

At first, relating to other kids was pretty easy—just place him with another toddler in a room with toys, and they seem to get along; that is until he or the other one wanted the same toy. But as he grew, he discovered that not everyone wanted to be friends with him. He discovered that relationships were hard.

From Standing Out to Standing Up

At school, kids made fun of him for multiple reasons, and he learned very quickly that others judged him based on his clothing, how he talked, and for some of his family's beliefs.

One time, he was in music class in kindergarten, when the teacher stopped the class during the transition between lessons and pulled him out of the room.

She knew his family was "religious" and pretty strict about what they "approved of" regarding music and other things. The next lesson included rock music, and she knew his family wouldn't approve.

To his embarrassment, he had to leave the classroom for twenty minutes, while the other kids were taught the lesson in "rock" music—songs by Elvis and other rock stars of the 60s and 70s. He stood out in a big way, and all the kids kept asking why he needed to sit outside of the classroom. He told them the truth—he was not allowed to listen to rock music, which caused another rift in the relationships with the other kids. More fuel for their ridicule.

It happened again a few years later when the kids in gym class were learning how to square dance. He was not "allowed" to dance because his family and church prohibited it. There are few things more embarrassing than a kid having to sit with his back against a cold gymnasium wall, listening to the music, and watching all of his peers learning how to do-si-do.

He became a pariah in elementary school, which was hard on him. Sure, some friends came alongside him and encouraged him, but more often than not, those friends acted differently when the "cool" kids were around.

While he did have a soft heart toward others, he was not afraid to stand up for himself. Like the time in third grade when one boy had been picking on him and challenged him to a fight after school. He hadn't done anything to this boy, but for some reason, he was targeted for this fight.

All day he was nervous and hoped to find a different exit from the classroom to escape the fight. Unfortunately, there was only one exit from the classroom, but luckily you could go in one of two directions once you walked out. He just had to pick the right direction. News spread to all of the third grade, and as luck would have it, both directions were blocked by a crowd of kids. There was no escape. It was like a fight-club scene on a miniature scale. He was surrounded on all sides by kids shouting, "Fight! Fight! Fight!" The kid who challenged him was on one side, while his friends were encouraging him to "beat him up."

The young boy told him he didn't want to fight, but the other boy kept pushing him and egging him on, trying to get a reaction. For some reason, this time of ridicule was different than all the other times. Perhaps he was just sick and tired of being treated so poorly by the other kids. Or maybe he realized he was at the point where if he didn't do something, the ridicule would never stop. It could have been the fact that his dad had always told him that fighting was wrong, but if he ever got to the point of having to defend himself, he shouldn't hold back.

Whatever it was that drove his decision that day, he decided to respond in force. The fight moved outside, and that's when he grabbed the other boy by his shirt and swung him around, letting go right at the edge of the hill that led from the sidewalk of the school down to the basketball courts. The other boy fell and rolled half-way down the hill. The crowd was surprised by the burst of energy from the "weak one." They couldn't believe it! Just then, a teacher rounded the corner and kids started scattering. The young boy escaped undetected.

Something in him changed that day. He discovered he didn't have to take the abuse. He could stand up for himself. And, the perspective of the other kids changed toward him that day. He didn't remember many times after that where kids targeted him for ridicule or tried to back him into a corner to fight him. He was still not the "popular" kid, but at least he was not verbally abused and picked on anymore.

He Is More Than What Others Said about Him

Being twelve-years-old was one of the most confusing times in the boy's life. Puberty. His mom invited kids from his class to his house for a surprise birthday party. He had not developed many close friendships with these kids, and even though he loved the party, he felt incredibly awkward around the other kids.

Also, during that same year, he discovered that dating girls was a way to make him feel good about himself. He dated one for seven months until she broke up with him on a yellow piece of paper with red handwriting. It simply said, "I don't want to go out with you anymore."

Middle school came around, and another young man began to pick on him in music class. After class was over, another burst of energy hit him, and he punched him in the chest knocking him over the chair behind him. He felt horrible after it had happened but also felt a little pride in the fact that he was more than what others said about him.

Embracing Pariah-hood

In high school, he was invited to a young woman's fifteenth birthday party where there was dancing. Because of his church's belief against dancing, he acted like he was hurt so he didn't have to dance. He sat on the sidelines as people came over to ask him if he was okay.

As a freshman, he was instantly recognized as the younger brother of the senior. He found it easy to develop relationships with others and never felt satisfied sticking to one group of people. Perhaps it was because he knew what it was like to be the outcast. He made friends in all types of cliques, gathering around himself others who struggled the same as he did. He had a great group of friends, and they spent a lot of time together.

It was at this time that he had his first serious relationship with a girl that lasted three years. He broke up with her when he was in his third year of university, and found himself right back into the mix of trying to figure out the rest of his life, what his purpose was.

If you haven't already figured it out, the boy in this story is me.

It wasn't until I was forty or forty-one when I discovered my real purpose in life. Through all of the different relationships, strict church upbringing, getting to know people from all walks of life and backgrounds, and struggling with my own insecurities (which I still struggle with even today), it became clear.

RELATIONSHIPS ARE MESSY

It takes a long time to figure out who you are, let alone how to be in a relationship with other people. There are so many worldviews, opinions, and stereotypes. Unfortunately, we are so divided as people. We allow our skin colors, backgrounds, belief systems, and views determine who we decide to agree with, spend time with, and be around. Our speech is laced with our own quirks, prejudices, and preconceived notions. We judge people based on our experiences and allow our minds to go to places they shouldn't without taking the time to get to know someone or letting that person's behaviors speak for themselves.

All of us have experienced the pains of ridicule or not been given the benefit of the doubt in relationships. I'm sure we have been on the side of judging others before we get to know them, and have been both burned by someone in relationship and burned others in relationship.

A non-scientific poll was taken on Facebook by mutual friends, and the question was asked: "What areas of relationship have you struggled in or have been burned by?" Over sixty responses came in a matter of twenty-four hours, in public or by private message.

When it comes to what people struggle with in relationship, the majority of the struggles center around communication and boundaries (establishing and maintaining them, whether those boundaries are their own or others). Trust is another issue that stood out. Others included humility, commitment, transparency, resentment, expectations, forgiveness, empathy, and being overly sensitive or aggressive.

People highlighted trust, respect, integrity, and authenticity as issues of impact when they were asked how they were burned in a relationship. Some were lied to, treated as inferior, abandoned, used, and weren't recognized when they gave of themselves. Not being noticed or seen was another issue for some people.

No matter how you look at it, relationships are messy.

SOCIAL MEDIA RELATIONSHIPS

Whenever you go out into the community, the store, work, school, or even just outside your house, you will be involved in relationship. We cannot escape it. All of us struggle with certain aspects of relationship with others.

Even still, some of the most meaningful relationships I have are with those where we have mutually done the hard work of communicating to gain understanding by listening to each other. Any time invested in those relationships has been by far the best way to continue to grow in friendship. But in today's culture, face time is a scarcity.

Without face time spent, we cannot expect to understand or be understood by others, which is the primary need that each of us has. This can and does get lost in the world of social media. We meet someone once or twice and then connect on social media. We can follow their posts and begin to think we "know" them because we see their life being played out in pictures and comments.

This has several pitfalls. One, people usually only post the highlights. It is very seldom that people show their true selves on social media. It is actually refreshing to see someone post something raw and emotional because of loss of a loved one or the hurt of a broken relationship.

The façade of "knowing" someone because we follow their posts on Facebook, Instagram, Twitter, Snapchat, and so forth, can be deceiving. There are some who get offended when they are not invited to a party because they are "friends" with you on social media and you actually know their brother or sister. There are still others who may think they have meaningful relationships with others just because they private message each other on a somewhat regular basis.

Social media is not bad. It is a connection to another human being after all, albeit a loose one. At the very least, this connection can become something valued when we actually spend time with them. The only caution is to not mistake a loose connection on social media for a meaningful relationship. We can become emotionally attached to the posts, videos, pictures, and status updates. This emotional connection may make it easier for a deeper face-to-face relationship, but we cannot mistake the emotional connection for a close friendship.

WHICH BRINGS ME BACK TO MY PURPOSE

This book contains my observations throughout my own life of what it means to "love your neighbor as you love yourself."

I consider myself a "student of relationship," but by no means would I ever claim to be an expert in relationship. If anyone claims to be an expert, then I challenge you to find the weak spot in their life, which lies with those closest to them. While we walk this earth, we will be ever-learning not just how to co-exist with other human beings, but to develop healthy, meaningful relationships.

When God gave Moses the Ten Commandments after the people of Israel left Egypt, all ten related to vertical and horizontal relationships. The first four were about a relationship with God, and the second set of six was about our relationships with each other. Jesus was often questioned by religious leaders trying to trap him. In one case, they asked him which of the Ten Commandments is the most important. His response was the following:

> "'You must love the Lord your God with all your heart, all your soul and all your mind.' This is the first and greatest commandment. A second is equally important: 'Love your neighbor as yourself.' The entire law and all the demands of the prophets are based on these two commandments." (Matt. 22:37–39, NLT)

These two commandments point us to a vertical relationship with God (love the Lord your God) and horizontal relationships with each other (love your neighbor as yourself). Churches do a pretty decent job at helping us understand the need for and importance of a relationship with God, however, it can be quite challenging to tread the ground of relationships with each other.

My purpose *through relationship* is to help others discover how to live out the second commandment Jesus gave. I feel it is my number one priority to discover, study, and teach how to love your neighbor as yourself. In some respects, it is a lost commandment—the lost art of relationship.

This book is my journey of discovery in relationship. As you read through this book and begin the archaeological dig to discover how to love your neighbor as you love yourself, I desire that you will see similarities of your life in mine and also learn the same lessons (or confirm those you have discovered) through some of the stories I share. I hope you will look back on your own life and think about your own life lessons and the people in your life who taught you what you know today. Digging into your memories is challenging and rewarding but worth it.

I encourage you to think about the principles we will cover in the context of everyone you come in contact with. This book is not a marriage-help book, dating book, or even a how-to-get-along-with-your-family book. It is about our relationships with all human beings who inhabit this world.

It's about rediscovering the *Lost Art of Relationship*.

2.

The Art of First Impressions

After a very long time spent looking for a relationship that would lead to marriage, I had all but given up. This was back in 1997 when the internet (AOL 3.0) was beginning to really catch on. AOL had a search bar where you could type in a keyword (in this case "Christianity") and go to a particular group who associated themselves with that keyword. On that landing page, there was a message board where people could communicate, "chat" back and forth and get to know people they otherwise would never get to know.

It was not meant to be a dating or match site, just a place to chat (almost like a prehistoric Facebook). There was a username on the message board that from a glance looked like a friend of mine. I clicked on the post, and to my chagrin, it was not my friend. It was a guy using the message board as a way to find women.

For me, first impressions are fragile, and most of the time I would hesitate to accept the first impression. However, some people lay all of their cards on the table and show their true colors right up front. That was this guy. He went on in his post to describe the "perfect woman" for him, even down to her hair color, eye color, and body measurements. He ended by saying, "If you do not match any or all of these criteria, don't even bother responding."

Thankful this was *no friend of mine*, I clicked out and saw there was a response to his post. My first thought (impression) was, "What poor woman would respond to this jerk?" Well, it was the woman with whom I am now married. If I had not clicked on her response to this guy's message posting, I may not be married to my wife or even sitting here writing this book.

She let this guy know that he would never find the right woman because he was only looking at the outward appearance. No self-respecting female would ever want to be around a pompous, self-absorbed man such as himself.

She was preaching to the guy and even quoted Bible verses to him! I admired her courage to speak up and tell it like it was, so I emailed her privately and told her so. That began a two-month email and phone friendship. We talked for hours on end (and the Sprint ten-cents-a-minute phone bills proved that). Two months later, I planned a trip out to meet her for the first time in person. It is not every day someone gets the opportunity for *two* first impressions, but I did.

When I first saw her, I was blown away by her outward beauty. And I'm sure she was blown away by my Caesar cut, gold chain, black shirt, and vest (said very *facetiously*). I was a youth pastor and associate pastor in inner-city New Jersey, and I did my best to look the part.

We went to a place called Solvang for the afternoon. Needless to say, my second first impression in person was not as much of a win as my first "first impression" over email and phone. We (she) decided we needed to start over as if we had never met before. I think I scared her. However, by the end of my week visiting her, I had won over her mom, dad, sister, and her. We have been married since 1998.

I am more than grateful Tania decided to let me prove myself over a period of time instead of taking her first impression and moving on to the next guy.

RELATIONSHIPS AND FRIENDSHIPS TAKE TIME

A really great friend of mine says getting to know someone takes four seasons at least—to go through four weather seasons and the seasons of life together before you can honestly feel you know someone. If you base your potential relationship with someone (and I am not referring only to romantic relationships, but *all* connections with people) on just a few short moments and then decide not to proceed in getting to know them, you may miss out on an incredible relationship.

We've all heard the saying, *"First impressions are everything!"* Not only did I hear this growing up—I actually believed it! Sometimes first impressions can be right on target. However, they are not one hundred percent and certainly not foolproof. Malcolm Gladwell, noted author of the book *Outliers,* was quoted as saying, "We don't know where our first impressions come from or precisely what they mean, so we don't always appreciate their fragility."[1] We should always do our best at letting people see who we are at a first meeting, but cautiously. If we fake who we are to make a good first impression, we can begin the troublesome road of deception. Be sure, the real you will come out eventually.

A caveat: You decide what you allow people to know and understand about you. This chapter by no means suggests you should hide the areas where you need improvement. Just don't lie about who you are.

Here are a few reasons, from my perspective, why first impressions are not as accurate as we think they are.

1. First impressions do not account for the circumstances surrounding the target of our first impression.

A person we meet for the first time could have had the absolute worst day with few things going their way. This may cause a negative feeling on our part because they avoided eye contact or showed ambivalence to our meeting.

Or, they could be elated from a recent deal they brokered, one in which they were dishonest. Upon meeting us, they seemed pleasant, friendly, and happy. The danger if we accept this first impression is that we may find ourselves cheated in a deal with them in the future and left wondering how he or she could have been so dishonest.

The fact is, any external circumstance can alter the emotions of a person masking who they really are. Some would say that feelings *are* a telling factor and should be considered with a first impression. That may be true to a certain extent. However, I would suggest emotions should only be taken into consideration if, after a trial period of the relationship, you see a pattern of behavior that indicates this person has difficulty separating their emotion from reality.

The other reason we could consider emotions after a certain period of time is if the person has difficulty balancing their feelings with the world around them, which *can* lead to issues down the road.

2. First impressions do not account for how *we* are feeling, or what preconceived notions we may have.

I have been guilty of not taking my own emotions or circumstances into account many times. After an initial encounter with another individual, I may draw conclusions about their character or personality, which could be based mainly on my emotions during the meeting.

We could have had the absolute worst day with few things going our way, which feeds into our reactions to new situations and people. We could have had family issues (sickness, problems with children, a death in the family) which are hard to mask, even if we put on a façade when meeting others for the first time.

As I have grown, it has become a much better practice to spend time with the other person, to get to know them better, and to allow their consistent actions and behavior speak louder than my ideas about them. Usually, someone's real character will come out eventually, at which time we can decide about whether we will continue to pursue this relationship-friendship.

There is an old lesson in the Bible that says, "Do not judge others, and you will not be judged. For you will be treated as you treat others. The standard you use in judging is the standard by which you will be judged" (Matt. 7:1–2). We have to be careful not to judge them prematurely.

3. Simply put, first impressions are initial feelings, not necessarily the truth about them or you.

Have you ever said something in the heat of the moment that you later regretted? Have you ever put your worst foot forward and wanted to go back and start over? Or have you been so caught up in your own life that you were oblivious to the lives of those around you?

Something tells me you said *yes* to one or all of those statements.

To be fair to others, we should allow them a second chance. We certainly desire second chances when we blow it. Keep in mind this is about building *healthy* relationships. There could be some people who manipulate you and leave you feeling confused. Chances are, they would continue to do so if you gave them a second chance.

To be fair, we need to look at all of the underlying circumstances surrounding the first encounter. We can ask,

- Where am I emotionally, and what is my situation at the time I will meet with _____?

- What happened during the day, or is happening in the other person's life, that could negatively affect our meeting?

- What could have been said about them or about me that possibly tainted either perspective before we met?

- If I believe I have received a second chance in my relationship with God, shouldn't I give others that same benefit? Am I willing to give them the benefit of the doubt?

SPIRITUAL APPLICATION

In Acts chapter 2, the disciples who followed Jesus were in the upper room when something phenomenal happened. God met them there and gave them the ability to speak in other languages.

Those who were outside of the upper room hearing what was going on with the disciples did not know who they were. They understood in their own languages what was being said, but didn't understand why. Those who did not understand and needed to explain it away wrote it off as drunkenness (vv. 1–13).

This is a prime example of a first impression going wrong. Fortunately,

Peter was able to command the attention of the crowd to explain what was going on. He debunked the idea of them being drunk since it was so early in the morning (vv. 14–41).

Pitfalls of First Impressions

Often, we are not given the opportunity to explain our actions after a first impression. We can be pegged as a particular kind of person or personality, and it can be quite challenging to come back from it.

This is unfortunate because some excellent people deserve a second chance in relationship. The question is, are we willing to treat others how we would want to be treated by giving others that second chance even if we were *not* given that same honor?

When we tell someone they need to do something to "impress" us in thirty seconds or less, we are basing our potential future on half a minute. It is impossible to know anything more than where someone came from and what they do for a living in thirty seconds. First impressions are so fragile. It is truly unfair to base a decision on pursuing a relationship with someone who may have had difficulty with that one chance to "impress."

This brings up another question—*who are we trying to impress?* If we are trying to impress someone, we leave the judgment in his or her hands. If we are trying to honor God in our relationships, we leave the judgment in the hands of the One who has the right to judge. God takes our relationships very seriously. How we treat others can say a lot about how much we value God's view of us. This is not just about first impressions; it is about the condition of our hearts and how we view others. What if God handled us the same way we treat others? Most of us...no, *all* of us would be doomed.

Why do we place so much emphasis on our "first impressions," anyway? Are we *really* that skilled at determining who someone is by the first few minutes we spend with them? I mean, we know that first impressions have *a lot* to do with what mood we are in when we meet someone. If you are happy when you meet someone, your outlook is brighter, and you may be able to assess someone in a shorter amount of time. If you are sad when you meet someone, the opposite may be true.

The concept of speed-dating is an excellent example of this. If you get ten to fifteen people of each gender into a room and give them three minutes to talk to each other, then ask them to assess which person they would rather spend more time with going forward, there are many factors in play that could skew the results.[2] First, although we were taught not to judge a book by its cover, we inevitably have a picture in our mind of who we would get along with based merely on their appearance. Second, in a few short minutes, what can you really find out about a person other than how they look or how comfortable they may seem in a social (albeit controlled) setting? Also, we should be cautious about first impressions. What if someone was there to deceive us? How easy would it be to get lured into a bad relationship because we looked at outward appearances?

There was another man in the Bible, Samuel, who went to look for the next King of Israel. In 1 Samuel 16, we read how Samuel went through the selection process. Samuel ultimately chose young David, but at first, Samuel looked at all of David's brothers, because all of them had exterior qualities that seemed more fitting for a king. However, God saw David's heart and his inner qualities of strength, loyalty, and honor; that's why He chose him.

Verse 7 says, "Don't judge by his appearance or height, for I have rejected him [Eliab]. The Lord doesn't see things the way you see them. People judge by outward appearance, but the Lord looks at the heart."

Many of us have heard that we need to perfect our "elevator speech" or we could lose potential customers or clients. A friend once told me of a story about going to a business gathering of owners and decision makers where each person was given one minute to tell the rest of them why they are "cool." Imagine how awkward it would be to stand in front of other people and try to explain all the things about yourself that you believe make you "cool"—in sixty seconds! I'm sure it was complicated by the fact that every person in that room probably had a different interpretation of what "cool" is to them.

I could give example after example of how we continually judge someone by our own perceptions of who we wish to be friends with. However, one of the best examples I can give is a story of two women and one church.

Two Women, One Church

I pastored a church in Culver City inside of Los Angeles for almost six years. It was a re-church plant. In the first week of pastoring this little church, a husband and wife were feeling like our church could be a great fit for them to get involved. I invited them out to dinner along with my wife. We met at a Marie Calendar's and enjoyed a nice meal together. During dinner, the husband and wife confessed that they were both unsure of placing themselves under the leadership of someone who was twenty-seven years old, a whole twenty-five years younger than they were.

Their first impression of my youth could have potentially caused them to move on to another church. My only response was to ask them to give me six months of their time. If they still felt the same way, I would hug them and bless them as they moved on to another church home. They did decide to give me a chance, and they became two of the most dedicated, involved, and giving people the little church had.

Another woman started attending our church. During services, she would shout out comments during my sermons. She was not familiar with church, or what it meant to listen, reflect, and study at home. She was from New York City, got right to the point, and shared her thoughts with no inhibitions.

The woman of the husband-and-wife team came to me and said, "Pastor, you need to do something about this woman! She is driving me crazy!" Even though I couldn't agree more with her, in my heart, I knew there was a lesson here. Not everyone that enters into our lives will come in ways we expect. From wisdom that could only have come from God, my response was to encourage her to take the New Yorker out to coffee or lunch and get to know her.

It turned out the New Yorker was the primary caregiver of a husband who was physically disabled and verbally abusive. These two women became good friends, and eventually, the interruptions in service subsided, and the New Yorker became a loyal volunteer and attendee.

OVERCOMING THE FAILED FIRST IMPRESSION

If humility is evident in our lives, then a failed first meeting and poor impression can be overcome. If pride is there, the failed first meeting is tough to overcome.

I can say, with certainty, that I need to be reminded on occasion to give people the benefit of the doubt. One way I do this is to personally take time to meet with them in a public setting. At that meeting, I usually ask them questions which lead them to share their life and faith journey—where they grew up and how they came to live and work where they are currently. It is incredible how much you can learn about someone if you just ask questions and take the time to get to know them.

When you show a genuine interest in someone's life, often it brings a reward—a good friendship. Hopefully, the interest in you is reciprocated, and God will be honored in the new relationship that has just formed. We will never know unless we decide to take it beyond the first impression.

Businesses are starting to understand the need to take someone out of a traditional interview situation, moving their interview to a restaurant. The purpose is to see how they handle themselves in social situations, how they address and treat the wait staff, and also how focused they can be on the conversation. This is an excellent test of character or social acumen. If you take someone out of a formal work setting, you start to see the real person come out.

Of course, this doesn't mean you will always be able to assess a person accurately. They may be incredible actors that can fake even a longer lunch or dinner interview. However, it is less likely to hold up under the pressure of time and social distraction.

LOVE YOUR NEIGHBOR AS YOURSELF

Our culture pushes first impressions mainly because we are thinking of ourselves and what someone can do for us, instead of what we can be and do for someone else, or possibly just wondering who they are as people.

How do first impressions change when seen through the lens of loving your neighbor as yourself? When thinking of yourself, you only want to give someone thirty seconds, because time is valuable and you cannot get it back.

When thinking of others and treating them how we would like to be treated, our view of the first impression changes. Give someone the gift of time to show who they really are. Allow them to make mistakes. Maybe you have been placed in their life to help them get to a different place, a better place, or vice versa.

Loving your neighbor as you love yourself teaches us to look at others as potential connections where we both mutually benefit, and others benefit as well. If we simmer down those initial starting points and base our future connection on just a short period of time (say, one to two minutes), we could be missing an opportunity to have a relationship that is valuable to both of us.

When Jesus walked this earth, He didn't take the preconceived notions of the religious over us. He showed us that first impressions rest in our hands to judge—and we are not that proficient at judging others by the outward appearance.

There is *no way* we can judge the heart of someone, either.

ONE FINAL THOUGHT

Why is it that we push the first impression?

Is it because we do not want to take the time to get to know them? Are we so busy on our own stuff (work, to-do lists, our agenda) that we force others into a thirty-second-to-one-minute time frame of pressure? Can we make a judgment in that short time frame about whether we want to spend any more time with them? It seems to me we have already made that decision when we force them into such a short assessment.

Those who are in higher positions do not need to meet with everyone—it is impossible; otherwise they may never be able to get anything done. However, when they *do* meet with someone, they should carve out more time than one to two minutes.

Don't underestimate your own influence and overestimate your instincts on people. Our instincts are just not that dialed in. Be intentional with those you spend time with and be honest up front. Just as much as you are making an assessment on another person in thirty seconds, they are also thinking the same thing about you.

Give your time.

Give of yourself.

Be intentional in your first impressions where you decide to be yourself and allow others to do the same.

3.

The Art of Service and Reconciliation

My mom passed away on October 25, 2006. I will remember that day for the rest of my life. There is not a day that goes by that I don't think of her.

That day solidified for me a lesson I had been learning for almost twenty years, but never fully realized it until several years after she died. I asked if I could speak at her funeral, which turned out to be one of the most difficult talks I have ever had to present.

It was a Wednesday, and I received a call from my sister. She couldn't even get the words out, so my brother-in-law, Jason, had to give me the news. The shock of that phone call sent me reeling. It was difficult to function, but I had to get my senses about me. My wife was in Maryland for her internship in oral surgery, and I had a six-year-old and a twelve-year-old to take care of, not to mention a business to place on hold.

It took me almost sixteen hours to get from Los Angeles to Baltimore. It was during that plane trip that I had an opportunity to think about my mom, her thirty-three years of influence in my life. I had a chance to process an event that would forever change what I thought about relationships.

A Lesson in Serving

For as long as I can remember, my mom was the last one to bed and the first one awake in the morning. I sometimes wondered if she actually slept. It was almost an unspoken expectation that Wynnelle Chrystal would answer the call to serve at church or in the neighborhood, and she was the one who got things done where she worked.

She always found ways to serve others. People loved her. She talked to anyone...I mean everyone literally! My father once told me she would talk to a wall if no one else would listen. She was one of the most relational people I have ever known. She knew how to strike up a conversation and ask the right questions to get someone to open up.

At family events, she made sure everyone was comfortable, had enough to eat, and that we all pitched in to clean up. My brother and I were often drafted into much of the work and effort she put into serving others, as well as my dad.

As I look back, I realize that she probably sacrificed more energy than she had to give. She didn't have an outlet to care for her own self physically, emotionally, or psychologically, short of talking to my dad and her sisters.

She loved children. She lit up when she could work with them. She became the Sunday School Superintendent, taught classes at church, and even worked her way up to Director of a day-care center, which served children before and after school. She lived and breathed serving kids.

At her funeral, hundreds of people were there. Many had not seen my mom for years, but countless people came up to me and told me stories of how my mom had influenced their lives and how grateful they were for our family sharing her with them. It brings tears to my eyes just thinking about it.

A relationship cannot happen unless people are willing to give of themselves to others—this was a significant lesson I learned from her. I can recount so many memories where I watched my mom place others' needs above her own. Serving and having the mindset of service can and will have an incredible impact on others' lives. They may not even realize it until you are gone, but the basic foundation of service is to do for others as you would want them to do for you. There is no expectation of how they will respond or whether they will reciprocate.

One thing is for sure...she loved others to a fault. She taught me to be keenly aware of the needs and emotions of those around me—to keep a watchful eye on the one who seemed to be isolated and find a way to include them. She taught me how to be a servant in relationships. The only thing I would have coached her to do differently is to make sure she spent time feeding her own soul and body, so she could have a healthy balance of service and refreshment.

When I finally got to Baltimore, I wasn't allowed to see my mother until the funeral home had prepared her for viewing. I walked into the funeral home, through the door of the viewing room, and up to the casket. At the precise moment when I saw her for the first time, I literally fell to my knees, broke down, and sobbed. The grief was almost unbearable.

There was this treasure of a woman who I was privileged to call mother, laying in a casket. I know all of the ways people encourage someone in that kind of grief and loss. However, nothing was going to bring her back.

I had a choice to make. Would I continue my mom's legacy and honor her memory by living the way she lived? Would I also learn from her mistake of not making sure her own soul was refreshed? (After all, one must learn to receive to give more, right?) The answers are a resounding yes. What she deposited into my life about relationships will stay with me forever, and I am reminded of it often.

FROM RELATIONSHIP TO RIFT

Things weren't always great between my mom and me, especially during my teen years. I remember three distinct times where we had pivotal moments in our relationship. The first occurred when I was twelve years old. We had a split-level home just outside of Baltimore, Maryland. Our basement was a half basement with a room my dad and Pop Pop (my grandfather) had built. I was laying on the sofa in that half basement watching TV. My mom had given me some kind of command, and I said, "NO!" As a good southern mom would understand, there was no room for disrespect in the mother-son relationship. Her reaction was swift with a hand coming toward me to slap me in my disrespectful face (which I deserved). This had happened before, and I deserved it every time. However, my reaction this time was very different. I reached up and grabbed her hand, stopping its momentum. She tried to pull her hand away, and I didn't let go. With that one action, I caused a rift in my relationship with her. Something changed in our relationship at that moment. I was stronger than she and I had proven it. Thus began a verbal struggle that lasted over many years.

It was not long after this when our family was driving in our Oldsmobile Cutlass Supreme to a destination I do not remember. I had talked back to my mom, and she reached back over the seat to try and pinch the backtalk out of me. She had been successful many times, but my wily agility allowed me to dodge every attempt. My mother looked at my father and tried to solicit his help. I'll never forget my dad's next comment. "Hon, he is getting older and stronger. You will not be able to discipline him this way anymore. It's not working." Even though I had been spared the physical discipline from them after that day, other areas began to close in on me.

Let me stop and say, as parents, they did the best they could with my brother, myself, and my sister. I didn't make it any easier for them to parent me. They were by no means perfect, and I definitely was not a perfect son. Through their strengths and weaknesses, they taught me so much about relationships. The way I was raised has made me the man I am today, faults and all. However, I needed to take responsibility for all of my actions, reactions, and relationships.

Whether it was night or day, or cold or hot outside, I don't know, but there was one day that will be forever marked by a comment she made to me.

What I do remember is that because of the progression of the two pivotal points mentioned earlier, my mom and I had started to argue...a lot. Between the age of twelve and just about fourteen, my rebelliousness had risen to new heights. It was difficult for my mom to control. In fact, she just couldn't.

We were in the heat of an argument (subject unknown). I had targeted my mother with rebellion. Maybe because she was four feet eleven and ¾ inches and I was growing to five feet and a half —I'm not sure. At the height of the argument, my mom said these powerful words...

"If you don't stop this bad behavior, you will never amount to anything!"

I don't know if you have ever been affected by a comment your mother or father made to you, but this comment has stuck with me for almost thirty years. Little did she know it would change me for the rest of my life. How I decided (and currently decide) to allow it to change me are entirely different. More on that later. This event, a momentary lapse in judgment and her saying something that scarred me for a long time, taught me so much about the need and importance for reconciliation in relationships.

You see, I had allowed this comment to become the focus of my life. I wanted to prove her wrong. That I *would* make something of my life. Any time anyone would even allude to the fact that I could not do something, it became my mission to prove them wrong. Sure, I accomplished things, but my motive was in error. T.S. Elliot wrote in *Murder in the Cathedral*, "The last act is the greatest treason. To do the right deed for the wrong reason."[3]

My relationship with my mother was wounded, and when I became an adult, we only talked when it was necessary. When I left home, I had no intention of going back to Baltimore. I moved to Pennsylvania for college, was recruited to inner-city New Jersey for work and ministry, met my wife and moved to California, got married with an instant family (my wife had our oldest daughter before we met), and my wife and I had a baby together in 2000.

Life was passing by, but my relationship with my mom remained wounded. The scab had crusted over, but never fully healed. I'm confident that all of my other relationships were affected by the lack of reconciliation in my relationship with mom.

FROM RIFT TO RECONCILIATION

It was September 11, 2001. We lived in Los Angeles, CA, in the UCLA family housing on the corner of Sawtelle and National Boulevards. My mom and dad came for a week-long visit with us, and dad flew back home on September 9 because he had to get back to work. Mom stayed a couple of extra days.

I was awakened at 5:30 a.m. PST by a phone call from my sister telling me to turn on the news. We all woke up and turned on the television to see what everyone else was seeing live. The first tower of the World Trade Center had been hit, and smoke was billowing out. Our jaws had dropped, and our hearts were broken for the ones who had lost their lives up to that point. We then watched as the second plane exploded into the second tower. I will never forget that day for as long as I live but not just because of the terrorist attack.

That tragic event sparked my memories. I began to feel, almost immediately, that I needed to reconcile with my mom for the comment she made fourteen years earlier, one in which I played a significant role in causing her to say. That night, still reeling from the 9/11 terror attack and the eeriness of empty streets and quiet skies, I decided to sit down with my mom and my wife and let her know about how the words she said so long ago were still with me.

After I had recounted that day fourteen years ago, my mom's countenance changed. She started to cry and said she didn't even remember saying those words, but was deeply sorrowful that something she had said in anger impacted my life so negatively. She then said the words that ultimately put me on a course correction in the relationship,

"Please forgive me, Danny. I never wanted to do or say anything to hurt you, and I am so sorry you have lived with this for so long."

Of course, I began to sob. I quickly forgave my mom and also asked her to forgive me for never coming to her sooner to make this right. That night, fourteen years of hurt was healed, and the journey of our reconciliation started a new path of relationship that brought us so much closer.

You see, Tuesday, September 11, 2001, was the day my mother was scheduled to fly out of LAX back to Baltimore at 11:00 a.m. PST. Who knows how deep the terrorists' plans were and how many airplanes were targeted? No one will ever know, but I could have lost my mom that day and would have never had the opportunity to reconcile with her.

I learned so much that day. Deep and meaningful relationships are always threatened when we put off reconciliation and forgiveness (to be covered in the next chapter).

I might have lived in regret for the remainder of my life if my mom had been on an airplane that was used as a weapon against the United States. Mom lived another five years after that. In 2006, she died suddenly of a pulmonary embolism that broke free from her leg and went straight to her heart. She was sixty-one years old.

During those five years, I grew so much closer to her and valued our relationship. The healing that took place because I decided to seek reconciliation freed us to deepen our bond. You just never know when those you are closest to, or even yourself, will be gone. Value these relationships now. Do not hesitate to love others, forgive others, and seek reconciliation. You won't regret it if you do.

4.

The Art of Forgiveness

Some not so good quotes on forgiveness:

*"Sometimes the first step to forgiveness is understanding
the other person is a complete idiot."*
~ Bill Murray (Twitter)

*"I asked God for a bike, but I know God doesn't work that way.
So I stole a bike and asked for forgiveness."*
~ Emo Philips

Have you ever heard the expression, *"I forgive you, but I will not forget"*?
There are still others that say, *"If you don't forget, then you have never really forgiven."* There are problems with all of these expressions.

For those who say, *"I forgive you, but I will not forget,"* I doubt forgiveness was really given. It sounds like a veiled threat. The next statement, *"If you don't forget, then you have never really forgiven,"* is impossible. You can never really forget what someone has done to hurt you. We were designed to remember. From the day we were born, our brains turn on the memory banks, and we retain massive amounts of information. When we are hurt by someone, or if we hurt someone else, whether intentionally or unintentionally, we remember.

Two phrases we should focus on more are,

"Please forgive me,"

and

"I forgive you."

Before we unpack the act of forgiveness, we must understand the bondage caused by unforgiveness.

CHAINS OF UNFORGIVENESS

> *"Unforgiveness chains us to the past, poisons the present and keeps us from what the Lord has for our future."*
> ~ Unknown

Chains are heavy. If you have ever carried a set of chains, you have felt their weight and also the relief when you put them down. Chains are used for many things, one of which is to confine, hold down, or keep someone or something within a certain limit. Many times, you will see chains on a prisoner in transport. Chains is a metaphor for bondage.

Like chains, unforgiveness is a weight we carry with us. We actually place ourselves in *bondage* when we don't forgive. The control we *think* we have, we have actually submitted to the person who is the *object* of our unforgiveness.

Living with unforgiveness in our hearts toward others will slowly dismantle any healthy relationship piece-by-piece. I have witnessed it destroy marriages, family relationships, friendships, and slowly eat away at the health of two of my own family members.

We have *all* been hurt or offended, whether it is something said or done directly to us, or indirectly (i.e., gossip, throwing us under the bus, and so on). Frankly, it feels horrible. Not one person I have met likes to be hurt or offended. There are those who are quick to be offended (who we would label as "thin-skinned"). I know, because I used to be one of them and I still struggle with this today. Thankfully, there was someone in my life who came alongside me as a mentor and taught me how to have thicker skin—who taught me about forgiveness. He showed me there are two responses to being hurt and/ or offended. Either we allow unforgiveness to set in because we choose not to forgive them, or we can release ourselves from the offense or hurt by forgiving them. When we don't forgive, it leads to five side effects of unforgiveness: *bitterness, distrust, insecurity, anger, and resentment.* Let's start with bitterness.

Bitterness

> *"Unforgiveness is choosing to stay trapped in a jail cell of bitterness, serving time for someone else's crime."* ~ Anonymous

Bitterness is a major side effect of unforgiveness. When we hold a grudge (bitterness), the only person who is really negatively affected is us. We continually remind ourselves about who and what caused the offense, opening the wound that was inflicted over and over again, never allowing it to heal.

I have seen bitterness literally begin to affect someone physically, causing sickness, headaches, and poor health. Yes, bitterness is a terrible thing. It is like a festering wound that never heals. It is a scab that when picked begins to remove the healthy skin around the wound. Bitterness causes someone trouble and begins to strain the relationships with those they are close to. Living with bitterness blocks us from truly loving others.

Distrust

> *"What loneliness is more lonely than distrust?"* ~ George Eliot

Distrust is another one of the significant results of unforgiveness. Anyone around the bitter person can be a target of distrust. The hurt or offense that planted the seed of unforgiveness, which grows into a root of bitterness, becomes the lens we look through, even with those closest to us. We can begin to think that everyone is going to hurt us in the same way. We believe we are the only ones we can trust and this inevitably leads to an exhausting and lonely existence.

Insecurity

> *"The reason why we struggle with insecurity is that we compare*
> *our behind-the-scenes with everyone else's highlight reel."*
>
> ~ Steven Furtick

Insecurity is an outcome of unforgiveness. We begin to believe we are the reason why we were hurt or offended—that no matter what we do, our situation will always end up the same. Insecurity strangles out the healthy aspects of any relationship, as we become emotionally unavailable to give or receive love or care.

Have I gotten your attention yet?

Unforgiveness leads to bitter people, who are those who have never let go of a past offense or hurt. Instead, they build up walls in their hearts, become distrustful of others, and allow insecurity to rule their emotions. Maybe they were hurt by...

a family member

a church

a pastor

a friend

an ex-spouse (or current spouse)

someone of another ethnicity

a co-worker or employer

someone in leadership

When offenses are not dealt with in a healthy manner, walls are built—huge walls.

> "See to it that no one falls short of the grace of God and that no bitter root grows up to cause trouble and defile many." (Heb. 12:15)

Bitterness can strain our relationships. We begin to see others through the lens of the grudge; distrust grows into a stalwart tree and blocks us from experiencing the warmth of other relationships. It is the root that grows to become that stalwart tree that cannot be moved. The only way to get rid of bitterness is to *uproot* it. It needs to be removed entirely.

Anger

> "Get rid of all bitterness, rage and anger, brawling and slander, along with every form of malice." (Eph. 4:31)

Unforgiveness can most definitely lead to anger, another side effect, which is a biological response to an external or internal trigger in our life. Some of these triggers may be the way someone says something to us (whether in an offensive way or bad tone), a betrayal, or simply a memory of a bad event in our life.

When the trigger is engaged, a chemical response happens in our brains, adrenaline is released, and we enter into "Fight, Flight, or Freeze" mode. Some of us instantly engage. Some of us avoid the confrontation. Still, others shut down altogether.

It is totally okay to experience anger. It's *not* okay to hurt someone in our anger. This is why I believe Ephesians 4:26 (NIV) was written, "In your anger do not sin." We *can* control our anger by learning the difference between reacting and responding.

For the most part, reacting to external stimuli doesn't take much thought. It is almost immediate. A positive example of reaction is when someone is about to walk into a pole; you see it and yank them away from the impending knot to their head. A negative example of reaction is reading an email, then writing a long diatribe and hitting send before you have taken time to calm down. I think we all know how well that works out...

Responding takes more thought. To respond to an event, a comment, or even a threat is more calculated than a reaction. We decide to do this, whereas a reaction is usually immediate. A response can be immediate if we have already thought through how we would react to a potential action toward us. There are multiple examples we could think of to show what it means to respond. However, let me throw a positive one your way.

Have you ever been in a relationship with someone (not romantic, but any connection such as work, family, or friendship), and the other person continues to say and do things that trigger an anger emotion? Of course, you have! According to Newton's Third Law, "For every action, there is an equal and opposite reaction." So our reaction says or does something equally with the same tone or with the same sharpness.

A response, however, takes a look at the circumstances surrounding the person causing the trigger to engage. We begin to think through and take notice of the other person and what they are going through. We also can take a look at what we may be doing to cause their trigger to engage.

Positively responding to this situation could be showing kindness, even though we may feel it is undeserved. Responding could also present a soft approach, asking the other person how they are doing, and /or what they are feeling. When we choose to respond, we have more opportunity to strengthen a relationship than when we react. That is, of course, if your response has the health of the relationship in mind.

If we continually "react" to stimuli that cause anger or other negative emotions, it can lead us to the fifth side effect of unforgiveness—resentment.

Resentment

"Resentment always hurts you more than it does the person you resent."
~ Rick Warren

Resentment becomes the thread which runs through everything we do. All other relationships are affected, and it blocks us from trusting others, getting close to others, and opening up our lives to others. Resentment is a relationship killer, as it spills over into other potential relationships.

Anyone who may fit the description of what drove us into resentment becomes a target for our negative emotions. When resentment becomes a thread interwoven into all other aspects of life, it can keep us from enjoying new potential friendships and dismantling existing relationships. Why? Because we replay the hurt and/or offense over and over in our minds and hearts. When we are reminded of a past hurt, we start this whole cycle of unforgiveness all over again. This cycle keeps us in *prison*. We are the ones who hold ourselves in bondage, in these handcuffs. We think we are in control, but unforgiveness means we have yielded authority to the person who offended us.

Breaking the Cycle

So how do we break this vicious cycle? It all can be broken by making one decision. It is not always an easy decision, but a high reward can come from making it. It can be summed up in one word—*forgiveness.*

"But, you don't know what they DID to me! You don't understand the level of the hurt or the result of the offense! Am I supposed to allow this person to continue to step all over me emotionally?"

You are right. I can only tell you in my own life what forgiving someone has done. It freed me to love again. It opened up the door to reconciliation on my part. Forgiveness shows another person the strength of your character, the depth of your love, and the power of mercy. There are still people in my life that are dear to my heart who have not reconciled with me. I have done what I can on my end to facilitate it, and I am continually reminded of the hurt and the issue. The response that gives me the most peace is to forgive every time I am reminded of the hurt caused.

Don't take my word for it. Let's look at a couple of Scriptures for counsel.

> "Do not bear a grudge against others, but settle your differences with them, so that you will not commit a sin because of them. Do not take revenge on others or continue to hate them, but love your neighbors as you love yourself. I am the Lord." (Lev. 19:17–18)

The law is being given to the Israelites in the wilderness. Healthy relationships were of paramount importance when you have a couple million people roaming the desert. Forgiveness breeds a healthy community.

Forgiving others is one of the commands that has lasted throughout time! It was not just a New Testament concept that Jesus brought to us in his ministry. Relational reconciliation was commanded long before, and it is recorded in Leviticus as well as in other parts of the Old Testament.

There are only a few of the Ten Commandments that instruct on loving God, but the rest are concerning how we treat others in relationship. Jesus took the Law and not only fulfilled it with his life and ministry, but he also taught deeper than the religious leaders ever could because he was the Author of the Law. He explained his original intent—matters of the heart and how we live in relationship with other people.

> "Then Peter came to Jesus and asked, 'Lord, how many times shall I forgive my brother or sister who sins against me? Up to seven times?' Jesus answered, 'I tell you, not seven times, but seventy times seven.'" (Matt. 18:21–22)

When I read this passage, I like to add a little inflection to Peter's voice as if he is exasperated. It can be compared to us getting frustrated that we have offered forgiveness, but the person who offended us continues to insult us. Jesus shows the nature of where our hearts should be when it comes to reconciliation.

This passage also tells me that we will always remember, at the most inopportune times, which we have been hurt by and how we have been hurt or offended. When we are reminded (and we will be), we are to forgive yet again as if it were the first time. Why? We are designed not to forget. Our brains are wired to remember. From birth, our brains retain information, and as we get older, we can recall this information because of a smell, a sound, or something we see or touch that reminds us of a past event, emotion, or even a hurt/offense. When we are reminded, it can trigger the anger emotion all over again.

Forgiveness is a powerful tool. In any relationship, you *will* need to utilize this tool if you desire to keep these relationships. It is difficult to understand the magnitude of the power of forgiveness if you do not realize the need for it and how it can help you develop deep, meaningful relationships. Forgiveness is not just apologizing and moving on. There is a difference between saying, "I'm sorry" (an apology), and "Will you please forgive me?" (forgiveness). Let's take a look.

APOLOGY VERSUS FORGIVENESS

I can remember a situation where I had committed to moving some boxes out of a room so another person who needed that space could prepare for an event coming up a few days later. I dropped the ball on my commitment and did not move them.

This person called me early in the morning and asked if I could come and move them as they needed the room to get set up. When I arrived, they had already been moved out of the room and were being transported to another location. I jumped right in and began to not only move my items but other items as well.

When I saw this person, I walked right over to them and could tell they were not happy with me. They tensed right up. I had a choice to make. Would I just say I was sorry, or would I go the extra step? What happened next was visibly noticeable.

I said, "I am so sorry for missing this. It was a drop on my part, and I should have moved them." Just as soon as this person was about to say something, I added another line, "Will you please forgive me for missing this one?" Their body language changed from "ready for the fight," to "please help us get the rest of the items moved."

Saying "I'm sorry" doesn't truly show remorse. Asking for forgiveness shows that we are taking responsibility for our part in the offense. It also indicates an understanding that the other party can and should contribute emotionally to the act of forgiveness.

Saying "I'm sorry" also doesn't require a response. We expect one, but it doesn't require one. When I say or do something that hurts someone's feelings, and I realize what I did if I walk up to them and say, "I'm so sorry for how I hurt you," I can expect them to accept my apology, but they are not required to receive it. I'm not asking them to do anything. I am merely acknowledging the wrong action or words and showing I recognize my offense.

If we are honest with ourselves, most of us expect a response to an apology and for healing to take place. When a response does not happen after an apology, we get mad all over again.

Asking forgiveness inherently requires a response. You are making a request. The person has a decision to make. Picture it this way: you have wronged a friend. It happens. You feel horrible because you never intended to hurt anyone. When the time is right, you ask your friend if you can talk. When they accept, you start by acknowledging the wrong. Then you proceed to let them know how you feel about hurting them. If you stop there, reconciliation is just around the corner, and you may miss an opportunity to deepen the bond of friendship. So, you don't stop there. The next and final step is to say the five words that break through the barrier of the wrong, "Will you please forgive me?"

At that point, your friend has a decision to make: forgive you or carry the hurt and live in their own bondage of unforgiveness.

When you forgive or ask for forgiveness, the weight of the offense and the responsibility is now off your shoulders. It frees you to trust others again, understanding that people are imperfect and so are you. It is not dependent on the other accepting or granting the forgiveness.

If you remember the story of my mom, you'll remember that reconciliation happened when the forgiveness was asked for and granted, with a recognition of the part both my mom and I had in the relationship.

My faith has been the best example to me of what it means to forgive. In my mind, it is easy to harbor bitterness. Then I am reminded of how much I have been forgiven. I have lied, taken jealousy to places it should not have gone, and failed others in relationship. Worse yet, I have been unable to follow the greatest instructions ever given: to love God and love others as I love myself. Breaking these commands has placed me in the category of someone in need of forgiveness by God. And Jesus bridged that gap in relationship, forgave me, and has shown me that it is possible to live in relationship with others, to have deep, meaningful friendships, and to love others as I love myself.

Right after Jesus gave the disciples an example of prayer, he made a statement that haunts me. He said this to his followers, which means that he takes this matter of forgiveness very seriously:

> "For if you forgive other people when they sin against you, your heavenly Father will also forgive you. But if you do not forgive others their sins, your Father will not forgive your sins." (Matt. 6:14–15)

Not only does forgiving others free you to live unhindered in relationship with others, but it also frees you to live unhindered in relationships with God.

This verse may sound confusing at first. If we ask forgiveness from God, why would He not grant it? Someone who has truly understood the cost of forgiveness from God, through His Son, Jesus, will know that if we can be forgiven from so much, we should forgive others for the offenses and hurts they have caused.

SIDE EFFECTS OF FORGIVENESS

Living a life of forgiveness has its own side effects that are much more beneficial to us—they are *sweetness, happiness, and joy.*

Sweetness

I am *not* a big fan of eating bitter foods! I drink sweet tea, sweet coffee, eat ice cream, and absolutely *love* sweet chocolate. Place anything in front of me that has sugar, a dusting of sugar, icing, and so forth, and I will most likely try it. What I have trouble with is bitter things—grapefruit juice, arugula, and black coffee are not my favorites. And may I add, bitter people, are not high on my list of those I wish to spend time with. Who really does? I say, no one.

Bitter people are not fun to be around. I have a term for them...EGRs... meaning "Extra Grace is Required" if you pursue relationship with a bitter person. Bitter people lose friends, and deep down their bitterness grows each time a relationship walks away.

You cannot forgive and maintain bitterness.

When you live a lifestyle of forgiveness, you just become sweeter to be around. You are less likely to leave a bitter taste and more likely to leave people feeling better about themselves. We become someone that others like to be around. We are less likely to live in judgment and high criticism of others, and we are also more likely to have people around us because sweetness elevates and attracts others.

Sweetness in our attitude and disposition, a genuine sweetness of a life that understands forgiveness, will eventually bring light into the lives of others and maybe even a smile to their face. Of course, you will always have others who wallow in their bitterness and inadvertently, or even intentionally, try to make you bitter as well.

Have you ever met someone that consistently maintains a calm demeanor? They take things slowly, try to see the best in others, and do not react quickly to adversity? They seem to have a positive attitude and show respect for others unapologetically. This is a person that has come to learn that responding with a clear head and kindness to someone who lives in bitterness can keep you from falling into the same bitter pool of emotions.

The only response that will help us rise above bitterness is to pray for them, continually forgive them, and treat them with kindness to the best of our ability. It can be difficult, but both the internal and eternal rewards will be sweeter.

Happiness

When you live a life of forgiveness, life becomes sweeter, and you have more opportunities to experience happiness. Happiness is a biological response to an external or internal trigger in our life. When the trigger is engaged, a chemical reaction happens in our brains: endorphins are released, and we enter into a "euphoric" mode.

When I have coached people, I will often say never make decisions when in any kind of emotional state, whether angry, happy, sad, or jealous. The reason for this is simple: when you are elevated emotionally, it is more difficult to operate in the logical and sensible decision areas.

People often mistake happiness as something other than emotion. Yes, you can experience happiness through a change of perspective, which is the point I am trying to make. However, happiness should not be a metric for how well your life is going.

I will be sad at times, especially upon remembering my mom's passing from this life. If someone says, "Look on the bright side, you will see her again someday," this does not make me feel happy. At that moment, sadness, also an emotion, can be healthy as I remember her. When I begin to focus on the legacy she placed in me for service to others, humility, and the ability to hum and sing for any situation, I start to experience happiness, and a smile comes to my face.

If we live in unforgiveness, we will focus our perspective on the faults in others and the areas of their lives that negatively affect us. We find it much more difficult to change our perspective and experience happiness around them. Noticing a beautiful sunset becomes difficult. Seeing the beauty of life becomes elusive.

The cool thing is, when you live a lifestyle of forgiveness, you are more likely to sense those moments that cause you to be happy and stop to "smell the roses" and the awe of creation. Happiness can come at a memory sparked by a smell, a sound, a touch, or by a present experience that causes you to stop and take notice of a blessing.

In relationship, you can use these times to strengthen your connection of friendship with others and share in those moments.

Joy

What is joy?

Some define "joy" as "a feeling of great happiness," "a source or cause of great happiness: something or someone that gives joy to someone," or "success in doing, finding, or getting something."

These definitions relate joy to a tangible object, or to an event. The trouble with these definitions is that if we look at it through our finite human minds, joy could be an elusive object that seems to evade our experiences. We would find it difficult to grab hold of, or it could slip through our fingers when we experience failure, loss, or any negative feeling.

To truly understand joy, it would help to go back to the Greek language to find the essence of the word. The Greek word for joy is *chara*, pronounced "*khar-ah*," with the emphasis on the second syllable. If you look at the definition at face value, it seems it would be the same as Webster's definition—"joy, gladness, source of joy."

However, let's break the word apart into its root meanings. The root of the word is *xar-*, which means "extend favor, lean towards, be favorably disposed." As is usually the case, a word can hold so much more meaning when we look at the root of the word and the essence of its meaning.

Xara (chara), then, means "the awareness of (God's) grace, favor, joy" or "grace recognized." There are a couple of other words in Greek that are connected to the same root: *xairo*, meaning "rejoice because of (God's) grace," and *xaris*, meaning "grace."

As believers, God leans toward us and extends His favor, and because Jesus came to His creation and died in our place, He is favorably disposed toward us. This fact alone should help us as we go through any circumstance. We can have joy through even the most difficult of situations because we recognize and are living in awareness of God's grace toward us.

If it were not for Jesus, God's grace personified acted out and displayed, we would find it very difficult to experience joy, as in fact, many people do.

If we understand this, it doesn't mean that we will never be sad. It says that in our sadness, we can be reminded of God's grace toward us and allow the hope of our eternal future to lift us above the circumstance and give us a different perspective—one of understanding that this sadness is momentary. We will not always be in this state. We can be, will be, and are in God's grace.

Joy is the awareness that God's grace is never far away. In fact, it resides in our hearts, in our minds, and in our lives. Joy is not a feeling. Joy is not just a perspective. Joy can be our reality when we recognize God's grace even when our lives and what is around us is crumbling.

Joy becomes the thread which runs through everything we do—all other relationships are affected, and it opens us to trusting others, getting closer to others, and walking through any challenge or victory. It helps us to navigate the hurts, neglect, and/or offenses that take place around us and to us. There is One who is closer to us than anyone can ever be. He was more vulnerable than anyone as he opened his arms on the cross, loved us to the point of death, but then provided the hope that guides our lives.

Joy helps us to see, as we are *aware of God's grace,* that we can provide the same forgiveness to others that were given to us.

FORGIVENESS IS A CHOICE

"And when you stand and pray, forgive anything you may have against anyone, so that your Father in heaven will forgive the wrongs you have done." (Mark 11:25)

Forgiveness is not an emotion or a feeling. Memories generate old feelings. Since we choose to forgive, we also choose to maintain that forgiveness by derailing feelings that may arise when reflecting on past hurts.

The only way to interrupt the vicious cycle of unforgiveness that leads to bitterness, distrust, insecurity, anger, and resentment is through forgiveness. Every time we are reminded of a past hurt or offense, we are at risk of entering that cycle all over again.

The answer is to forgive again.

We can choose a lifestyle of forgiveness that says, "I refuse to dwell on this because I have chosen to forgive." It is true that forgiveness will stunt the growth of the unforgiveness seed. It can uproot bitterness and open the door to deeper relationships with others. We can prune the leaves of anger that grow and are sustained when fed with resentment by choosing to forgive.

Forgiveness is a *lost art,* one that can provide wonderful results when exercised. According to an article written about forgiveness and health by doctors at Johns Hopkins Medicine, "Studies have found that the act of forgiveness can reap huge rewards for your health, lowering the risk of heart attack; improving cholesterol levels and sleep; and reducing pain, blood pressure, and levels of anxiety, depression, and stress. And research points to an increase in the forgiveness-health connection as you age."[4]

We can face obstacles and relational challenges with confidence when we live a life of forgiveness. Just remember that unforgiveness yields a *bitter perspective*; causes us to *distrust* others; leads to *insecurity*; provides more opportunities to live and act on our *anger*; sews threads of *resentment* in our relationships. But forgiveness yields a *sweeter* perspective, provides more opportunities to experience *happiness*, and sews threads of *joy* in our relationships.

Let's learn these two phrases and practice them with each other.

Please forgive me.

I forgive you.

5.

The Purpose of Relationship

We're getting to the big questions, such as "What is the purpose of relationship?" This question alone could potentially take an entire book to unpack. However, we can state the foundational purpose of relationship in a couple of short paragraphs, but first, we have some other things to cover, if you will indulge me.

We see throughout history the causes of broken relationships: pride, vanity, arrogance, racism, narcissism, self-importance, power, lying, cheating, stealing, jealousy, ineffective communication, control, and the list could continue for several pages.

Just take a mental inventory of the broken relationships in your own life, and you will begin to understand what I mean. What was the root cause of the brokenness, whether you were the cause or someone else? Chances are the relationship could have been saved or still could be mended with some humility (or a lot) on both sides.

We have struggled for years in relationships. There are so many differences that divide us, whether culturally, racially, socio-economically, politically, philosophically, and so forth. Why do we even try to connect with others with the potential for all of these issues and conflicts? Why even bother? I have some ideas about this. Understanding why we humans need to connect with others will help us to understand the purpose of relationship.

Four Reasons to Connect with Others

When I first moved into the city we now live in, my whole goal was to connect with others, since we knew no one—absolutely no one—in Northern California. I found myself spending more time trying to convince people that my motives were purely to develop relationships and that I wasn't trying to sell them anything or get something from them.

Then I realized something that caught me by surprise. There are *reasons* to connect, which are simple and not all that mind-blowing. I came up with four of them which I believe if we are truly honest with ourselves and others, ring true. They are significant because they free us to be ourselves and to set the stage for openness, and hopefully, a quicker avenue to trust.

1. The relationship benefits me.

Why would I want to spend the time doing something if it doesn't benefit me? Oh my gosh! This sounds so selfish! It may seem that way, but follow me for a second.

If I ask to grab some coffee or lunch with you, the basis of my request is my desire for some time with you. This alone benefits me. If I can hear your life journey and know more about where you came from, who your family is, and how you came to be where you are right now, then I am benefitted. I now have a bit of knowledge about you. Just focusing on someone else for any amount of time helps me see beyond myself.

I also hope it will gain me a new friend. There is no way to tell if this is the case after the first time we meet, but I cannot find out unless I take the first step and spend some time with you.

Connecting with you may also benefit me with an expanded network of connections. The more people connect with, the bigger the web of support I have, which is made up of people with different skills and abilities—it grows exponentially.

When we treat others how we want to be treated, it begins with me but doesn't end there.

2. The relationship benefits you.

If something doesn't benefit you, why would you want to spend the time to do it? All of the reasons from the first point apply here as well.

I need to bring something to the table in this connection to you. The golden rule is to *treat others as you want to be treated.* One would hope that the new connection is not one-sided (although I will admit, not everyone is altruistic and not every connection will be reciprocal).

During the very first time you connect with someone, you will also share your life journey with them. This allows them to get to know you, where you came from, and how you happened to be where you are right now. Connecting with me should benefit you as you will also have an expanded network, potential support, and people with differing skills and abilities that can enhance your life.

My role in your life should now be such that when I meet someone who may need your specific skills or can address what you currently need, I may connect them to you. The bottom line is, I cannot benefit you if we do not connect.

If we stopped here, we could be tempted to think, "Well, we have established a great connection!" However, this connection only solidifies when this new relationship benefits others—the third reason we connect with others.

3. The relationship benefits others.

When we turn our new connection into a relationship, it is at that moment when we decide to bring our networks together to benefit someone else. It cannot just be for our own mutual gain.

When I expand my network through a connection with you, you may be the person who could assist and help someone that I know. I can become the bridge between your abilities and someone else's need. This also works very well in reverse.

Or, when we pool our resources together, we can focus our efforts on helping someone outside of our circles of influence that we may not otherwise be able to help. This happens when we reach outside of our own physical boundaries and dedicate time and effort to serve a need in our community or even around the globe.

The point here is that as we make connections with each other, it should and will work for the benefit of someone else. We were never meant to live only for ourselves. Have you ever wondered why it feels so good to meet a need that someone else has? You know that feeling you get when a smile stretches across the face of someone whose need has been provided for because you and another person worked together to bring it to them? Some organizations are designed for this purpose. Rotary International has the catchphrase, "Service above self." The idea is that every Rotarian will see the needs of their community and globally work together with other Rotarians to fulfill those needs to make a difference in the world.

There is one more reason to connect with others.

4. The relationship pleases God.

God created us to be in relationship. He meant for us to help each other. We were not designed to be alone, nor to isolate ourselves from the world. We shortchange our own lives and we shortchange the life of someone else when we believe we don't need others and the world doesn't need us either.

Relationship is God's second and greatest commandment to us—love others as you love yourself. You cannot obey this command if you never connect with others. Connection pleases God.

THE PURPOSE OF RELATIONSHIP

Finally, we get down to the purpose of relationship. In one word, it is *companionship*. This is the purpose at its very core. There can be various levels of companionship, such as family members (husband, wife, children), friends (hobbies, shared interests, fun), workmates (a shared purpose), or teammates (a shared goal). Whatever the level of relationship, the hope is that we will continue to increase trust, build on the connection, and find fulfillment in it.

In the process of finding this fulfillment of companionship, something happens—the need to connect on a deeper level rises to the top. We will inevitably try to find a way to build on what connects us. Sometimes this is successful, and sometimes it is not. Why do teams fail? It probably has something to do with a lack of relationship. Why do families fall apart? It probably has something to do with a discrepancy in relationship.

A companion is someone you share experiences with. Therefore, the reason you enter into relationships is quite possible to share experiences with others, to bring meaning to your life, and to come to a place of trust and understanding. This is why it is so devastating when someone breaches a relational bond; it can become more difficult for someone to connect with others when trust is broken.

Take a look at just one area—your work team. At work, you cannot escape it, you *will* be around people. If you are around people, you *will* be forced to interact. When forced to interact, you *need* to make the decision to be a valued part of the team. When you make the decision to be a valued part of the team, others *will* be drawn to you. When others are attracted to you, that means you *are* already part of a relationship—a team relationship.

What kind of team member will you be? If you connect with others in a meaningful way—with the purpose of bringing value to the team and to others—companionship will develop.

But what about that person on the team that only seems to be concerned for themselves?

Great question! The short answer is that it will slow the team down unless the team decides to address it. The key here is addressing this behavior. If you are the one leading the team, try having the team do a group activity. This activity should be intentional and focused on the team's ability to work together and value the contributions of the others. The expectation cannot be that the team members will become lifelong friends and therefore solidify the team forever. However, the hope should be to tap into the desire for others to be known, seen, and recognized.

If we dig deep down into our thoughts and feelings, we desire companionship to be accepted, to have friends, to feel valued, to make a difference, to be noticed, and to be seen. All of these desires can only be realized in the context of relationship with others. There is something deep-rooted in us that desires companionship with others.

I have met and talked to many people who had as their goal to "make it to the top." One common thread among the ones who didn't value the relationships in their life was the realization that they didn't have any meaningful friendships. What good is it to rise to the top of any field or any ladder if you cannot share it in some way with those you have gathered around you to share life? What good is it if you do not have companionship with others?

This may be difficult for some reading this book, as you may be a "get-the-work-done" type of person. I am especially challenging you to stop, look around at the people in your life, and take time to be present with them. Go ahead and strive to be the best at what you do. Just remember, being the best at what you do includes as a vital part of the equation...valuing others, developing companionship and shared goals, and an expanding relational capacity. And may I add that relationship can cause us to grow as people? It's true! Through friction, conflict, and adjusting to different personalities, we can experience positive growth and gain depth in our lives because of them.

Throughout our lives, it is so important to cultivate purposeful, intentional relationships. It is common in those over the age of sixty-five to struggle with loneliness and a lack of meaning and purpose. Retirement causes a loss of relationships, and many retirees miss the socialization aspect of the workplace. Also, families tend to put those who are retired on the backburner. Many go back to work solely for the sake of connection and companionship with others. They have to find ways to connect with others.

The challenge is this: begin to develop relationships that grow from acquaintances to meaningful connections—the true purpose of relationship. Become one who strives to improve your relational capacity to enhance your existing and future relationships—this will undoubtedly improve your life, your work, your leadership, and well...your contacts.

6.

The Art of Relationship

We get so comfortable with our current relationship setup. It takes an effort to make new relationships, doesn't it? Or, we withdraw into our own bubble of relationship because we don't want to take the risk of getting hurt or rejected.

This book is not meant to dive into the psychological areas that keep us from relationships, but to open up the mind to possibilities of meaningful relationships beyond what you believe you are capable of.

How many people walk by you every day and you have *no idea* who they are, what their story is, what brought them to where they are, and who they have in their circle of influence? What might happen if you take a chance and force yourself to meet a total stranger? Go ahead, do it!

> (DISCLAIMER: The author takes no responsibility for who you choose to try this experiment with, nor can he be responsible for the outcome, whatever that may be—unless you gain a meaningful friendship, and then I'll gladly take credit!)

There is literally *no end* to the number of connections we can make in relationship with people around us. We may say it's a small world, but is it really? With billions of people in the world, can we ever stop the cycle of meeting others? Not easily. So if the goal is to connect with others to develop meaningful relationships, how do we do that? It begins by understanding the levels of relationship.

Eight Levels of Relationship

One of my favorite things to do is to meet someone and spend time hearing their story; specifically, I like to understand where they were born and what brought them to where they are currently in life. I am not always successful in getting to that point with someone, because they need to be willing to share their story. However, what I have found in meeting people and developing relationship is that there are at least eight different levels that each connection may go through on the road to developing a deep and meaningful relationship. The first four build on each other, but the last four are all about getting to know someone.

1. Notice them

Yes, the first step in any relationship is as basic as knowing that someone even exists. It may be that you notice a person from across the room or they walk down the same street at the same time you do every day. Maybe the person works at your office or church and passes your line of sight and you "notice" them. You may have even been in the same church, neighborhood, or work environment for years and not noticed them until you became intentional about noticing them and now you do.

Other people can help us notice others too. We learn about a person through another friend or acquaintance, and the purpose of them informing you of their existence is because they think it could be a strategic relationship or just one that could be mutually beneficial.

This is the level of relationship where you know *of* someone. If the bits of details and information intrigue you just enough, then you go to the next level of relationship.

2. Meet them

This level takes a bit of effort and perhaps even some bravery on our part. Just because I have seen or heard of a person, does not mean they have seen or heard of me. Or they may have heard of me and already developed a preconceived notion, most likely in error. I am not really sure if the introduction would be welcome, but I know that to move forward with the relationship, meeting them is critical.

This can be quite difficult for some to do. Our fears can overtake us, depending on our past, our confidence, or our feelings. However, moving forward means that we must overcome these fears and insecurities, or else we won't be able to establish new relationships really. (If you find you are having trouble in this area, it would be best to seek help from a counselor, pastor, or a mentor to work on this.)

The types of fears that can keep us from moving forward are rejection, feelings of insecurity, inadequacy, or even fear of someone knowing you have these fears. After noticing someone and assessing the value this person could potentially add to your life, take the risk! Push away those negative thoughts and jump in with both feet! Call, email, or just walk up to this person, reach out your hand, and introduce yourself. You have nothing to lose here but much to gain. Just remember, you should be able to add value to their life in some way as well; this is mutual. Simply put, just *start the conversation*. As this happens, you automatically enter into the next level of relationship.

3.   Acquaintances

The word acquaintance literally means "a person's knowledge or experience of something, or one's slight knowledge of or friendship with someone." This level is strictly surface knowledge and based on experience with them. You may have had coffee or lunch with someone. You do not really *know* this person. You only know some things about them.

An acquaintance is not someone I would place a significant amount of trust in at this point. You have crossed the threshold of relationship and broken the ice. You now know *of* each other and may slightly know *about* their background and current life, but unless you are an expert at interrogation, you really only have a small chance of knowing if this person has misrepresented themselves or if they are genuine. You are not even sure if they are really interested in you, or you them! If you are going to pursue a deeper connection (business or personal), then the next level is critical in helping you decide how far the relationship will go.

4.   Testing

Usually to get to this level means you have common ground with them or you will mutually benefit from the relationship. This is the level that probably takes the most time, attention, emotional investment, and care. The goal of this level is to get to *know* them, which takes time spent talking, working, and testing.

As you interact, you will notice clues and cues that will either raise a red flag or encourage you to spend more time getting to know them. No set amount of time works as a formula in this level. How long this takes is up to you and the object of your newly forming friendship.

My advice is to turn up the heat slowly. You need to move at a pace that the other person is comfortable with. And the other person needs to be open to it. There has to be a desire by both parties to continue the pursuit of friendship. It will not work otherwise. This is why paying attention to cues is imperative. Some of these cues are a lack of reciprocal communication, a glance away when you walk past them, or stopping a conversation with someone when you walk up. There have been many times in my life where I have been complacent, unaware of the signs, and was burned. Don't get burned like me. You can know beyond any doubt that the forming friendship will be tested at some point. Expect it and pass the tests. It is better to interact in person. Online and emails do not count. I met my wife on AOL back in 1997. However, we quickly realized that to get to *know* each other, it needed to be through communicating voice-to-voice, and eventually face-to-face.

The relationship will continue to be tested throughout its duration, whether months or even years. But to continue on, you have to enter into the next levels, getting to *know* who they really are.

5. Get to *know* them

If at the last stage, you didn't experience any significant red flags and you both have determined to move forward in the relationship, this is the point where knowing each other begins. You never really stop getting to know an individual. Why? Because, as time goes on, you both will mature as you experience different things or you enter new life stages and so on. Your relationship will change too as it grows and ebbs and flows. It is inevitable that you and the other person will have to adapt to certain situations.

Also, people usually do not lay all their "personal cards" on the table at the beginning of a relationship. There may be areas they continue to hold close to them, and over time they may reveal them to you. This comes down to how transparent the person is, which usually comes down to a level of trust. More trust, more revelation.

This is the stage where you will begin to understand what kind of life this person leads, who they really are, and what makes them tick. What gets them up in the morning? What do they enjoy? What frustrates them? What kind of hobbies do they have? What are some of their pitfalls? What do they define as success in their life? What kind of friend or relationship do they need? What are the goals they have set for themselves? And the list can go on. The key here is to discover "what" are they all about.

Knowing what a person is about is all part of understanding who you are adopting as a friend, a companion. There will likely be many similarities between you, whether it is an opinion, history, philosophy, faith, culture, life stage, and so forth. You will also discover traits or characteristics you are not in agreement with, so when you do find these, you decide as to whether you will just accept a negative quality or try to influence this friend for the positive. **Just keep in mind** that your friend must know this negative trait exists in their life and they must desire to work on it or change it. Otherwise, trying to change someone who doesn't want to could cause a rift in the developing relationship. We must remember we are becoming vulnerable to them learning the negative things in us as well, and they too get to decide what they want to accept or not. This works both ways.

6.   Know *why* someone is the way they are

At this level, you start (and continue to learn) about *why* this person does life the way they do it. Why do they respond in specific ways to specific events or circumstances? Why is it they may react positively or negatively to the same situation that someone else may generally react the opposite? Why do they think the way they do?

This level is where you have the realization they are what and who they say they are; a level of trust has been established, and you enjoy them. It may be common for you both to finish each other's sentences, or for you to be able to speak on behalf of that friend because you know how they may respond. **If you do,** do so with great care. A mistake here could set back your relationship or even stall it.

You have reached a level of familiarity and comfort with one another as you have had more experiences and time together. You are getting to understand why they do the things they do and you are good with it. It's more than likely you have already started calling them "friend."

7.   Someone you can call "friend"

Here is where there is a revelation of the nature of your relationship and the feeling that as long as you both maintain healthy communication and boundaries, you could be friends for a very long time.

We will dig into friendship in the next chapter, but a friend is someone who accepts you just as you are but is not afraid to call you on your issues. There is a trust that has grown to the point where you can share personal and confidential information and believe it will stop there. You can also rest assured they will not judge you for your actions, but share their opinion in love to give you a healthy, balanced view of you. Mutual accountability is very much a part of this level.

We throw the word "friend" around *way* too often. Many refer to some relationships in their lives as friends when they are actually still at the acquaintance level. "Friend" is a term that should only be used when it is mutually understood that this is the nature of the relationship. There is nothing worse than when you view someone as your "friend" and all this it implies, but they don't view you the same way. It has probably happened to all of us.

If there is a mutual friendship, a friend at this level will sense when something is amiss in your life. When you are down, they know it. When you are happy, they celebrate with you. When you are sad, they listen and allow you to cry—but not for long. When you need a push, they provide motivation. When you vouch for your friend, you believe they will represent themselves in an honorable way, knowing that your own reputation is on the line when you call them a friend.

At some point, and no one can really say for sure when this happens in any relationship if at all, you may move on to the highest level of relationship—*family.*

8.   Someone you can call "family"

Someone you can call "family" is someone you can do life with where the boundaries are all but removed. Sure, you still respect the relational boundaries, but truth, honesty, opinions, issues—*nothing* is off the table for discussion here.

You know that even if you yell, get into a disagreement, or become separated by circumstances or miles, you would be there for each other. If it is possible to be there in person, then you do it. But if not, you are there for them emotionally. Miles should *never* be an excuse not to pick up a phone and talk about your feelings, circumstances, issues, or to pray together. After all, you are family!

"One loyal friend is worth ten thousand relatives."
~ Euripides

Some people in our lives describe the family as only those who are blood-related or married into. I would like to blow that definition right out of the water. Sure, being blood-related or related by marriage technically makes you family. But it does not mean you have developed a deep and meaningful relationship that has been tested through all eight of these levels.

For example, I found out one summer that I have a cousin whom I have *never* met. I just heard about her and saw her on Facebook. We are not at the highest level of relationship just because we have a common bloodline. It will take time, face-to-face connection, and a mutual desire to walk through the levels of relationship.

I am still and will always be a student of relationship. As you read on, I will dive into certain aspects of relationship by sharing stories of people who have influenced me and taught me by their actions and behaviors. These are people who I have allowed to impact my life in profound ways. One of these areas is true friendship, which is what I want to share with you in the next chapter. Let's continue on the journey!

7

The Art of Friendship

*"A real friend is one who walks in when the rest
of the world walks out."*
~ Walter Winchell

I remember a particularly tough time in my own relational journey. Fortunately, I had a couple of friends that became emotional supports for me. Just knowing they knew what was going on was amazing. The fact that they walked with me through those dark emotional moments and didn't leave me to struggle on my own was incredible. They knew just what I needed.

As a student of relationship, it got me thinking about questions such as, what makes a friend? When do we begin to call someone a friend? How do we know we are still friends? Why do we need friends?

These are all excellent questions, some of which were answered in the previous chapter. One of the best ways for us to have friends is for us to understand, learn, and practice being a good friend. In this chapter, I explain five aspects of a friend that I think will help us with this. When reading through it, though, try not to think about how *someone else* needs to hear this.

These five aspects of a friend were taught and modeled to me by one of the greatest friends someone can have. They describe who a friend should be, what a friend should do, and how a friend should act. I mentioned before that I think we rush into calling people "friend," without truly understanding the implications of what it means to be someone's true friend. I hope this chapter will clarify this and help you as you continue to develop friendships throughout your life.

1. A friend *connects* and shares life with you.

"Because we loved you so much, we were delighted to share

with you not only the gospel of God, but our lives as well." (1 Thess. 2:8)

We were never meant to be alone. The Bible tells us, "It is not good for man to be alone. I will make a helper suitable for him" (Gen. 2:18). We were made for relationships so we can share our lives with other people—our hurts, dreams, disappointment, successes, and so on. But friendship takes connection; it takes reaching out to others, which can be difficult for many people.

Brené Brown, Ph.D. is an American Scholar, author, and public speaker, who is a research professor at the University of Houston Graduate College of Social Work. She gave a TED talk on the power of vulnerability. Through her research, we can learn some fascinating things. She gave us two reasons why we don't connect with others: fear and shame.

Fear in relationship believes if someone gets to know me for who I really am, they will reject me. For some of us, this comes across like this: "I'm fine alone. I don't need other people. I've got this. Leave me alone."

Shame in relationship believes, "I'm not enough—I'm not good enough; handsome/beautiful enough; talented enough; knowledgeable enough in Scripture; I'm not _____ enough."

The trouble with this is that connection takes several things. It takes:

confidence—believing you are who God says you are;

authenticity—letting go of who we think we should be to be who we really are;

vulnerability—embracing your insecurities and weaknesses; others have them too, so it is easier to connect;

humility—a breakdown of pride.

If we wish to have friends, we need to be willing to connect with others. This means taking a risk, as anything worth having will have some level of risk attached. The danger, of course, is whether the other person we are trying to connect to wishes to reciprocate that connection. We cannot control how others will respond, but we can control whether we try or not. We can also work on our confidence, our authenticity, our vulnerability, and our humility that make connecting much more natural.

We are all connected in some way. Sitting on a plane, in a classroom, in church, at work, standing in line at a grocery store, walking in your neighborhood, living in the same town, coming from the same state, having kids—all of these are starting points that help us to connect with people at the most basic level. They are entryways to a relationship. They are connection points. The only thing keeping us from walking through those entryways is a decision to engage.

2.   A friend shows emotion on your behalf.

Two of the greatest teachers that ever walked this earth is Jesus Christ and the apostle Paul. Throughout their ministries on this earth, they displayed or taught the care of others, and the role emotion plays in friendship, mainly these three:

Compassion is a deep awareness of the suffering of another living being accompanied by the desire to bring relief. Showing compassion is not just emotion on its own; it requires action as well. When you recognize the hurt, pain, sickness, or sadness of someone else and you do something to alleviate their suffering, you demonstrate compassion. This is a crucial connection point that will develop and deepen the friendship. It shows that we are not self-absorbed only thinking of how our relationship with someone affects us but solidifies in their mind that you care about them. People sometimes just want to know that others notice them and care.

Jesus showed compassion for people many times throughout his ministry, as we see in Matthew 14:14, "When he went ashore he saw a great crowd, and he had compassion on them and healed their sick." (See also Matt. 9:36; Mark 1:41, 6:34) Notice that in all of these instances, Jesus felt compassion and then acted. He demonstrated the compassion he felt for them in tangible ways.

Anger is a biological response to an internal or external trigger. The kind of anger regarding friendship I am talking about isn't spewing anger because we did not get our way or because we are upset with something that someone did to us. I'm talking about righteous indignation, the kind that Jesus displayed in Luke 2:13–16 and again in Matthew 21:12–13 when he went into the temple to pray and found the temple's outer courts filled with people exchanging money for animals to sacrifice. In my opinion, Jesus knew the noise and commotion made it very difficult for the worshippers who had come from long distances to focus in prayer—those who were not allowed into the inner courts because they were not Jewish, so he unleashed on the money changers.

If Jesus is our example of righteous anger, what do we do when someone takes advantage of a friend? How do we respond when a loved one is hurt by someone else? Are we outraged when an injustice or a crime happens against a friend? Friendship mandates that we get angry and we show that emotion on their behalf.

Grief is another emotion that friends display when it is appropriate. Many of us don't like to show sadness or grief publicly, as if it is a sign of weakness. I say, showing sorrow or grief publicly takes a strong person. If Jesus can be "strong" enough to prove that he cared, so can we. We can cry along with them just like he did in John 11:33–36.

> "When Jesus saw her weeping, and the Jews who had come along with her also weeping, he was deeply moved in spirit and troubled. 'Where have you laid him?' he asked. 'Come and see, Lord,' they replied. Jesus wept. Then the Jews said, 'See how he loved him!'"

Likewise, happiness should also be displayed when called for, just as Paul taught in 1 Corinthians 12:26, "If one part suffers, every part suffers with it; if one part is honored, every part rejoices with it," and Romans 12:5, "Rejoice with those who rejoice; mourn with those who mourn." These verses tell us that if one of us is going through a difficult time, we suffer too right along with them. If one of us is celebrating a win, we celebrate with them. Doing so shows we are willing to take on the struggles, pain, and difficulties of our friends, as well as be happy when things go right for them.

In these ways, the connection we have with each other goes deeper. Displaying emotion is part of true friendship.

3. A friend sticks with you, especially when the going gets tough.

> "One who has unreliable friends soon comes to ruin, but there is a friend who sticks closer than a brother." (Prov. 18:24)

> *"Fake friends are like shadows. They follow you in the sun,*
> *but leave you in the dark."*
> ~ Unknown

We will all go through dark moments or even dark seasons. Those are the times when friends double down on the friendship—to be there for each other. Think of a time when you were going through an extremely dark moment in your life. Who was there with you? Who stuck with you even though it was difficult? When you are pressed down and surrounded on all sides, who still sits with you, cries with you, and helps you? These are friends.

My wife and I took a tour of a cavern in Murphys, California. At one point in the tour, all fifteen to twenty of us were on a platform with about three or four small lights illuminating the space. The tour guide gave us the disclaimer that if we were afraid of the dark, we might wish to climb back to an area that was lit. No one moved. She said to imagine only having a candle to light your way—and she proceeded to turn off all but one light that was the brightness of one candle. It was dark, but we could still see enough around us to let us know where we were and how to get out if we needed to.

Then she took it a step further. She told us that if our candle went out, it would be like this. Then she turned off all the lights in that space. It was so dark that we could not see our hands directly in front of our face. It was not as troublesome, because we knew there were fifteen to twenty people around us. My wife and I were huddled next to each other, and I could feel the warmth of her side and the touch of her hand. We didn't panic and were comforted just knowing the other person was there.

There will be times in our lives where it seems so dark that we cannot navigate on our own through the cavernous troubles that surround us. We cannot see the danger, nor the way out. A friend can become the light that will illuminate our path or give us comfort in the middle of the darkness. Just knowing they are there makes the circumstance a little less troublesome. If a friend has been through a similar dark time, they can help navigate through the darkness of our circumstance to get through it.

A friend doesn't leave you there alone but sticks with you, especially when it is tough. They don't just stay with you; they speak into your situation as well.

4. A friend tells the truth—they wouldn't just watch you fail.

> "As iron sharpens iron, so one person sharpens another." (Prov. 27:17)
>
> "Wounds from a friend can be trusted, but an enemy multiplies kisses." (Prov. 27:6)
>
> "Perfume and incense bring joy to the heart, and the pleasantness of a friend springs from their heartfelt advice." (Prov. 27:9)

There may be a time where you have to tell a friend the cold, hard truth. It is possible to tell the truth in love, and it is also possible that in so doing, your friendship may be tested. If the friendship is true, then it will stand the test.

If we sit back and watch someone fail, knowing we could have done something to help them, is that really friendship? Or is friendship giving the other all of the options, facts, and truth, and then being there with them in their success or failure?

We have all failed. For some of us, we had a friend that tried to speak into our weakness to help us overcome it. We may have even pushed them aside and became angry with them. After we made it through the failure, hopefully, we looked back and saw how they tried to help us avoid it. And I'm sure we went back to thank them as well as asked for forgiveness.

"Brothers and sisters, if someone is caught in a sin, you who live by the Spirit should restore that person gently. But watch yourselves, or you also may be tempted." (Gal. 6:1)

"If your brother or sister sins, go and point out their fault, just between the two of you. If they listen to you, you have won them over." (Matt. 18:15)

Both of these verses give us permission to be a friend to others, to tell them the truth in love, and even potentially spare them from the consequences of a failure. Friends need to consistently and gently remind us of the areas we need to improve, too.

5. A friend will sacrifice for you.

"And the second is like it: 'Love your neighbor as yourself.'" (Matt. 22:39)

"My command is this: Love each other as I have loved you. Greater love has no one than this: to lay down one's life for one's friends." (John 15:12)

Act of Valor is one of my favorite movies. The acting is not perfect however it paints a very clear picture of the power of sacrifice.

In one particular scene, several soldiers are carefully advancing into a warehouse to take out the enemy. The team finds themselves in a room that has a vulnerable point, and they are on high alert. The enemy tosses a hand grenade into the center of the room. The chief, who is at the back of the team, sees the grenade hit the floor. In just a second's time, the chief notices the other soldiers do not see the danger, and without thinking of how this will affect his life, makes the decision to jump on the grenade to save their lives.

Even thinking about this sparks emotion for me. The thought of giving my life for others is one that has crossed my mind several times. What would I do in that split second? Would I be capable of making the same decision? I hope I would. However, there are many other ways to sacrifice without having to give your very life.

We can sacrifice our time to be there for a friend. We can sacrifice our finances to provide for a friend. We can sacrifice our own desires to help make a friend's dream a reality. There are many ways to sacrifice ourselves for another, especially for a friend.

"A new command I give you: Love one another. As I have loved you, so you must love one another. By this, all men will know that you are my disciples, if you love one another." (John 13:34–35)

Our connections and relationships will have lasting influence and could potentially change the course of someone's eternal life. Just like the possibility of a butterfly's flapping wings could prevent or cause a tornado, if we could tweak our perspective just a little, we have the potential of impacting the lives of those around us exponentially, especially through friendship.

We must understand that we are connected to each other. In the verse above, Jesus commands us to love one another. If one of us suffers, we all suffer. If one is honored, we all party alongside the one who is honored. This connection is how others can find hope. They will see how we are connected, and we can use *that* as an entryway to start a relationship with others.

What we *feel and do* has an impact on those around us. It is up to us to choose to influence them positively. Here's your challenge: practice all five aspects of friendship with those who are already in your life that you call a *friend*. Then, begin to show them to those you do not know, starting with connection. Let your emotions and actions be a catalyst for life change in someone else's life.

8

The Art of Transcending Differences

Growing up, I remember thinking that my dad was very strong. He went to work in the morning, sometimes before we got up, and came home around dinner, or sometimes very late when I was already in bed.

He was a grocery store manager for ACME stores in Maryland (if you're old enough, you remember ACME being in the Wile E. Coyote and Roadrunner cartoons). I never exactly knew what he did when I was younger, but I do remember that ACME stores had decided to close down their Maryland locations, and that meant my dad and mom had a decision to make. Would they move to Pennsylvania or Delaware where he would get a pay increase, or stay in Maryland, lose his position, and have to look for work somewhere else?

Because my brother and I were still quite young, they both decided it was best not to move us from our home to another state. They wanted us to keep our current friends, school situation, and neighborhood house. We lived on a dead-end street where every neighbor knew each other and would be there to help each other.

I remember one winter when Maryland had a major snowstorm where over twenty-four inches of snow fell in one day. The next day, being locked into a dead-end street where snow plows dared not tread (we were always the last street to plow), the entire neighborhood came out with their snow shovels and cleared the road and cars. This is such a vivid memory for me and possibly one of the best examples of a community coming together for a common purpose.

My father spearheaded the charge from our house, and my brother and I were drafted into the snow-shoveling army. It felt great! Yeah, I was tired beyond belief after that day, but the bonds made for our little dead-end-street community were sealed even more that day.

Once the decision was made to stay in Maryland, there were a whole new set of issues. My father was out of work for almost six months. Things were tight, but my parents never made it seem like we needed anything. My dad looked for work, went out almost daily to find a job, and filled out applications with subsequent interviews.

Whether right or wrong, my dad chose to keep the family in Maryland and placed himself in a tight position. We could have lost our home. We may have had to move anyway, but at least we were all around our support system. It helped that our extended family on my dad's side were all within an hour of where we lived.

As most children do, I have graphic memories of specific moments in my childhood. Some of them are good and some not so good. One such memory was hearing racial jokes in the house. It was mid- to late-1970s, and the civil rights decisions of the 50s and 60s were set, but there were residual behaviors that stayed long after.

I can remember hearing the "N" word in my house, especially when one person, in particular, would come to visit. I was young, but I remember thinking that I could not understand why anyone would think or act this way. We are all just people in the end.

My father searched and searched for a position in many different grocery stores. There was one that finally offered him a job in management. The name of the store was Super Allied (name changed for privacy) run by a CEO named Edward Kerns (name changed for privacy). Mr. Kerns, as my dad would call him, was a good man who provided a position for my father, saving our family from what would have been a tough road, if not for the income.

Mr. Kerns was an African American. My father, when hired, was the only white manager on staff and would remain the only white manager during his entire tenure there. My father did not divulge much of the following information until I was much older. The first day he met Mr. Kerns, he walked right up to my dad and said, "I guess someone may have told you by now, I don't like white people very much." To which my dad replied, "Give me six months, and I guarantee you will not have any problems with me."

He never did have any further issues with Mr. Kerns. As a matter of fact, there was mutual respect and admiration that blossomed between them. My dad experienced a change in his life, in his perspective, and in his relationships. Some of the friendships that arose and developed with those of a different ethnicity became some of the closest he would ever have.

Even though he had developed meaningful friendships with these men, at the customer level, he wasn't treated with as much respect. He told me stories of working in several of the Super Allied stores, where he was cussed out, using every profane word to describe his whiteness. Many people treated him very poorly because of the color of his skin. This experience completely changed his perspective. Being the only white manager in a predominantly black working culture gave him a taste of what it is probably like for a black man in a mostly white society.

I would not understand this until much later in life, but watching this as I grew into a man strongly influenced my behavior, worldview, and certainly, my life's work. I experienced my father embrace others of a different skin color and begin to develop deep and meaningful friendships with many men and women who looked different than us. My dad was respected and included in this work culture. He recounted with me on occasion that some of the closest friendships he had were with men from Super Allied. This position provided for the family until I was long out of the house.

While this position changed my father's viewpoint, subsequently it changed mine as well. Because of his example, it became easy for me to accept, befriend, include, and even champion the backgrounds and people who looked different than me.

Mr. Kerns retired after some time, and another man named Obadiah Schmidt Jr. had taken over the Super Allied local markets. My father was not only able to keep the level of respect with the new CEO but also became very close friends with him.

Two other great men became pivotal in my dad's life—Quentin Murray and Ted Knox. They befriended him and gave him counsel that allowed him to grow in his relationships. Many years later, my dad still gets together for lunch with these men who played such a huge role in his life. Not only that but when Super Allied closed down because of national chains taking over, Quentin Murray, who had since moved on from Super Allied, was vital in my dad moving over to another manager position at another supermarket, Food King.

The racism my dad endured during some of those days was incredibly difficult. It could have driven him into hate and separation, but the relationships he developed and still has today became the example to me of what it means to treat every person with respect and dignity. His example to me of humility and perseverance in relationships has influenced my life and has shaped some of the topics in this book.

He served others even when they were pouring out profanities to his face because of what he looked like. He learned the art of forgiveness and the importance of not holding a grudge—two essential aspects of relationship necessary to live a healthy life.

I encourage all of you to lay aside whatever is in your past that may have disillusioned you to relationships with those outside of your own color or ethnicity. You may find these new relationships will become the closest you will ever have. I know I have seen this to be the case, and I desire to continue to teach my children and grandchildren that heaven will be the most multi-cultural place you will ever experience, a place where segregation is *not* an option.

The point of this chapter is this: *relationship transcends external differences*. My dad's decision to embrace those who looked different than he set me on a path of intentionally seeking relationships with those who look different than me. Wherever I go, I realize that the relationships I can enjoy with someone who is black, brown, or any other color, is way more important than the differences between us.

9.

The Art of Encouragement

We arrived in Los Angeles on July 27th, 2001. My wife had been accepted to UCLA's dental school, and we were starting an entirely new chapter in our lives. With two kids, one was just turning seven and the other just eighteen-months-old, it was a challenge, to say the least. Fortunately, the house we had purchased in Orcutt, a town on the Central Coast of California, sold for a lot more than we had paid for it. The money helped us move to L.A., closing the financial gap between when I could get my business up and running.

I had resigned my credentials as a pastor temporarily so I could raise my kids and work. But I volunteered as much as I could at every church we attended. I developed some good relationships, including the one with the senior pastor of Pacific Christian Center in Santa Maria, Rick Bloom.

It was through Rick that I had decided to renew my credentials in ministry before I went down to Los Angeles. We knew no one in L.A. when we moved there. We truly were rebooting in a new area, city, and culture. We needed to get settled, start developing relational connections, and find a church!

When our oldest started school in September at Redeemer Baptist School, we were invited to an open house. One of her new friends was a little girl in that school whose dad was a pastor of a local church in Culver City. We met the pastor and his wife at the open house.

That night when Tania and I got back to the apartment and settled the kids in bed, we both looked at each other and said almost simultaneously that this little church was the one we would begin attending—sight unseen. That has never happened to us before or since.

We did just that. The church was meeting at a school. We attended the first service there and discovered they were at the end of a building-fund campaign so they could rent their own space in Culver City, which was already in the works.

As soon as I expressed interest and mentioned I was a pastor, I was thrust into the volunteer mix right away. They needed a worship leader. So, even though I had just started self-teaching the acoustic guitar, I became a fill-in worship leader. We began to meet and spend time with several people from the church on a regular basis, and I helped to retro-fit the church building along with other key volunteers.

Almost six months into attending there, the senior pastor resigned his position. His leaving threw this little church of about one hundred people into an extremely difficult season. Within one month, the attendance had dropped to twenty to twenty-five people. The church had signed a four-year lease with a lease payment of $4,400/month, and there was no pastor. They were in dire straits.

The district I was credentialed with that oversaw this church plant called me. Here is the kicker. The area director who oversaw this area, Fred Cottriel, had a mutual connection with me. Fred was the uncle of Rick Bloom. Rick had already given him a heads up that I was moving down to that area.

Through that relationship, I was asked if I would be willing to become the senior pastor of this church re-plant of now eighteen people, four of which were my family. There were seventy-five dollars in the church bank account, and even though I had an agreed-upon salary, I would not get paid until the fixed costs were covered with a surplus.

Enter Steve Preston.

My first board meeting included Fred Cottriel and three other gentlemen who were the sectional leaders where this church was located. Steve Preston was one of them, and he was the sectional presbyter (main leader) at that time. The first meeting was held at his church in the upstairs offices. That was the first of many meetings I had with Steve.

Steve is very relational, encouraging, and a mentor that I will always be grateful for. We met at breakfast restaurants to talk, build the relationship, and perform business. I walked into the restaurant with a baby stroller, my two-year-old, and a diaper bag; I sat down and tried not to be too distracted.

Steve was incredibly patient, and he genuinely cared. With Tania gone a lot due to dental school, a business that was picking up momentum, my being the primary caregiver to two little girls, and now the senior pastor of a church struggling to survive a difficult season, Steve became the one I went just to download stuff. I shared pretty much anything with him.

He heard my frustrations, my hurts, my happy moments, business successes, kid struggles, and everything else you can think of. Over the five-year period, before we moved out of Los Angeles, Steve had become one of the closest friends and confidants someone could have.

That first year as senior pastor of that little church was one of the most challenging years I have experienced. I think I might have resigned at least three times. Each time I called Steve as he was the one who directly oversaw this church and told him I didn't think I could do it anymore.

After a good night's sleep and a talk with Tania, I called back and pulled my resignation. Each time he said he had held it and didn't intend on turning it in. He knew that I had the potential and could power through the issues I was facing. He also knew God was more than sufficient to meet my needs.

This was the year I truly understood the verse in 2 Corinthians 12:9, "Each time he said, 'My grace is all you need. My power works best in weakness.' So now I am glad to boast about my weaknesses so that the power of Christ can work through me."

One sunny Saturday afternoon between Christmas and New Year's Day, I gave Steve a call. I was incredibly frustrated with some issues the church was facing, which had grown to about forty to fifty people strong. I was ready to throw in the towel again. But this time Steve reacted way differently.

After I had finished my diatribe on why doing this wasn't worth it, Steve clearly knew this was the time to respond firmly. I will never forget what he said. "Dan, are you a leader or a follower? If you want them to change their behavior, you need to lead them to change their behavior. Get to know them personally. Be there for them when they need it. Help them to understand how much God loves them. But *stop* complaining about the ones God has given you to lead!"

It was the slap in the face I needed to snap me out of my selfishness as a leader and turn my focus over to the ones I was leading—to care about their lives, to build a relationship with them, and to love them as I loved myself.

Proverbs 27:6 shouted at me,

"Wounds from a sincere friend are better than many kisses from an enemy."

There were countless things that Steve taught me through his friendship and leadership. We developed a meaningful relationship over the years, and he truly was there for me as I hope I was there for him during some of the most trying and painful times in his life and ministry.

Here are a few things I learned from my relationship with Steve Preston.

THE POWER OF ENCOURAGEMENT

It wasn't until several years after I had left Los Angeles and moved to Maryland, where my wife attended an oral surgery residency when I realized the power of encouragement. I had always tried to encourage others, but I learned how to master it through my friendship with Steve.

There is an art to encouragement. Steve and I had spoken over the phone several times in that few years after I moved to Maryland, and each time he would say something that left me feeling uplifted, strengthened, and resolved to persevere.

His encouraging words were more than just lip-service. *He had been there with me in the trenches of life and waded through the strong currents of ministry.* He stuck by my side and helped me navigate some difficult labyrinths.

When he told me how much of an example I was to him, I was more than humbled. I felt unworthy of his words but strangely comforted by them. He told me that when he went to train other pastors of church plants, he used my story as an example to them of how to overcome and stay committed to the task God had assigned.

When mastering the art of encouragement, it is so much more meaningful when it comes from someone who you have built a relationship with first. His encouragement meant so much more to me because of the relationship that he had taken the time to develop with me. Sure, you can encourage someone you barely know. However, the idea here is to understand the importance of the weight your encouragement carries when you have proven to be a friend even through the toughest circumstances. When you walk *through* the fire with a friend and encourage them in the heat of trouble, your encouragement can become a lifeline for them.

This is one of the reasons I believe Jesus came to this earth. He walked, talked, lived, and died through life's moments. He understands what it is like to struggle. He walks with us through the most difficult and painful parts of life. His life, death, and resurrection carry so much weight behind them and become the encouragement and hope for our present and future.

Who needs you to walk with them through the fire of life and struggles of ministry? Who can you encourage today because of your relationship with them?

Steve taught me the art of encouragement. He taught me to say what is on my mind not just to think it when it comes to lifting someone's spirits. I had allowed too many times to pass me by when I thought of an uplifting word I could share with someone. It is one of the reasons that even now, I will stop what I am doing when I think of a friend to text them and let them know I am not only thinking of them but praying for them right at that moment.

Consistency and Perseverance

Have you ever talked to a friend about the same issue over and over and felt as if they will never get it? You have given the same advice time and again and they still come back to you with the same issues? Well, that must have been what it was like for Steve at first. I must have seemed like a basket case to Steve at times.

Through his perseverance and consistency in our relationship, his example finally broke through. Sometimes it took unwavering patience. Other times he needed to slap me on the back of the head verbally. It is one of the things I so appreciate about Steve. He took the time to walk me through my hard-headedness and guide me through the dark rooms of uncertainty because he had already walked them and knew where the potential obstacles were.

He never gave me an ultimatum. He advised me on what course of action he thought I should take, but never judged when I chose to go a different way. Instead of assuming the worst when I made a mistake, he cared for me personally and where I was in life.

When we take the time to become friends with someone and develop a meaningful relationship, we need to make the choice that we will stick with the relationship and persevere even when it gets to the point where we feel "we don't need this."

This is one of the reasons, in my opinion, why marriages suffer so much. Once we get to a difficult spot, we throw up our hands and say, "I don't need this," or "I am not happy anymore!" When we say these comments, the focus is solely on us. If we placed our attention on the relationship—the "we" and not the "me"—we make a daily decision to persevere through most issues. We need to make the decision to be consistent in our relationships. If we act one way around one person and an entirely different way around someone else, we are not only inconsistent but lacking authenticity. At this point, there is no real relationship, just deception.

The relationship is worth more than the differences we see in others.

Steve was consistent with me and taught me how to be consistent with others even when they were going through something I could only guide them through. This does not mean we will not become frustrated even to the point of giving up. This is when perseverance comes in as we muster up the courage and resolve to stay in the mix when we want to throw in the towel.

Jesus was consistent and persevered. If it weren't for his consistent sin-free life and perseverance through an excruciating death on the cross, there would be no resurrection, and we would not be able to have the close relationship with

God we can experience now. His perseverance in life and through death brought about the awe-inspiring reward of an eternal relationship with him—offering us and everyone a *hope* that we could not possess otherwise.

Steve's consistency and perseverance in my life offered me hope to make it through the difficulty, and I did. My friendship with him became that much stronger because of it, and now the reward of relationships with others through what I learned is far greater.

HONORING FRIENDSHIP

The word honor has lost its influence in today's world.

To honor (v) is "to regard with great respect."[5] Honor (n) is "a keen sense of ethical conduct."[6] Honor is others-focused.

If someone honors friendship in this sense, they are placing the friend relationship in high regard and strive to be aware of their conduct around others. This takes practice and discipline. Mainly, it means that we tame the fire of the tongue and our urge to say things that can be damaging to others.

Honoring friendship is building others up, verbally, emotionally, and relationally. It also means when you talk about your friend to someone else, you hold confidences, never slander them, and speak well of them.

Steve taught me this through the most unlikely way. We were in a conversation (as we try to do every three to six months). He was overseeing church planting in the southern California district of the Assemblies of God and held workshops and seminars to assist those who were in the process of starting a church.

I was looking for resources I could add to my arsenal so I could consult with pastors in Northern California. It was in this conversation that Steve said in passing, *"I use you as an example when teaching these pastors about church planting,"* which I mentioned earlier. This simple comment he made to me accomplished several things.

First, I was more than affirmed and encouraged after many years of being removed from the church re-plant in Los Angeles. Just the fact that he considered my story to encourage and teach other pastors honored our friendship. Expressing that to me meant more to me then he will ever know.

Second, when we develop friend relationships with others, we seek the best in them and learn from it. As it says in 1 Peter 4:8, "love covers a multitude of sins," and in 1 Corinthians 13:5, "it does not keep a record of wrongs." Honoring friendship means that we work through the wrongs the other person may have done and then celebrate the best in that person. This is done in public and in private.

Third, as we continue to develop new friendships and connections, how we have treated others and how we have lived our lives, in private as well as in public, can determine the depth or level of relationship with them. As we honor current and past friendships with the new ones we are developing, you will find your community deepening and expanding in wonderful ways.

REBUKE WITH PERMISSION ONLY

Is it possible to speak the truth without leaving a mark, to express it in love where the other person (although stung) receives it and applies it? The answer is a resounding *yes!*

If you have ever been on a playground, you've undoubtedly experienced young kids playing all around you, while the parents watch and enjoy a few minutes of rest on the sidelines. Inevitably, there is a parent that wants to tell you how you should raise your kids. I'm sure you have either observed this or have been the target of it.

Here is the scenario: your two-year-old, who is still learning social skills, doesn't like something on the playground, so she picks up some sand to throw it at another child. Both parents jump up and run over but for different reasons. You run over to find out why your two-year-old threw the sand and to teach her that throwing sand was not an appropriate response.

The parent of the child who was the target of the sand runs over and rebukes you for not teaching your child proper playground etiquette. Instantly the hairs on the back of your neck stand up, and now you want to throw sand at the other parent!

Rebuke, when it comes from a stranger or someone you barely know, will give rise to defensiveness with little to no resolution. A rebuke from a friend who has walked with you and you with them through trials, who understands you and possibly how you feel and loves you anyway, has earned the right to speak into your life, even a rebuke.

There is no question that a true friend has your best interest at heart, and they only want to help. Don't get me wrong, just because someone is a friend does not mean we will automatically accept their rebuke. The rebuke happens, we react, then we think about the situation and remember their words. Their words may have had some sting to them, but just like a wound that needs to heal and causes pain in the process, so are the words of a rebuke from a friend. It hurts for a little while, but it is necessary to heal.

Steve taught me through his relationship with me that to speak into someone's life, I should not presume I have that right. I need to develop the relationship with them and prove my loyalty, love, and commitment to the relationship first. Even then, I still will ask for permission to speak into their life.

I also give permission to those closest to me to speak into my life. You see, we choose who we are going to allow to speak into our lives. Others do the same. To be given the opportunity and privilege to speak into another's life is a great honor and should never be taken lightly. It requires humility in a relationship. It requires us to be intentional and disciplined in what we say, how we say it, and to judge our motives for why we need to say it. It also requires trust.

Prove Confidentiality

How do you prove confidentiality? It takes time and trust given at the right moments. It also requires testing. This is not a game. If you can keep confidence for a friend, you will earn their trust.

I wouldn't start off sharing the deepest darkest secret you have with someone. Start small in this regard with your relationships. There is only *one* person who truly keeps all things confidential, and you can trust that he will always have your back. That is Jesus, of course. You can go to him with anything, and he hears you.

Still, others can be tested and proven faithful in their confidentiality. Steve did just that for me over the years. I can count on five fingers those whom I have shared some of the closest things to my heart, Jesus and my wife excluded. Four of them are still living, and the other went home to be with God several years ago.

I had arrived at a point where I needed to take a risk in these relationships and open up to share something that I would never share with just anyone. These were issues that I needed and expected complete confidentiality.

How did I know they could be trusted? How did I know they would not judge me or my situation? I didn't fully know. But I knew that each one of them proved to be faithful as a friend in and trustworthy in their confidentiality. To this day and beyond, they will always hold a special place in my heart and will always be in my prayers.

Steve has taught me so much in his example, his love for God, and his love for me. If you allow yourself to develop deep and meaningful relationships, there will be great rewards, and they will change your life—for the better.

10.

The Art of Vulnerability

It was the summer of 2009 when I met Gavin Brown. He was single, had graduated from the same Bible university as me, and now worked where I worked. When he first came to Trinity, he moved in temporarily with the worship pastor at the church where I was the Administrative (Executive) Pastor. For the first year we worked together, we just attended the same meetings, but we had not spent much personal time together. We had not developed a common ground or trust yet.

Gavin loved to have fun. Few people did not know who Gavin was, and if you met him, you would understand why. He is as outgoing as they come. He likes to include everyone, and when he is around, there will be laughter, honest conversation, and inquisitiveness that opens the door to understanding.

I wanted to get to know him better, so I asked him to lunch (or coffee, the details escape me). However, I do remember Gavin mentioned he wished he had taken the time to get to know me when he first arrived. We had mutual friends from Valley Forge University, some that he had come to know in different circles.

Over the next four years, we shared many times of laughter, conversations, and acceleration of friendship that became a reprieve from the craziness of ministry and relationships where we worked and ministered.

One of our favorite places to go for lunch is a restaurant in Lutherville, MD, called Bertucci's. For less than ten dollars we could get a fantastic lunch, endless salad, and fire-baked rolls that are to die for! Don't forget the olive oil and spices to dip your rolls in. At first, we spent an hour or so getting to know each other, but with each visit, the conversation would open up to more profound thoughts, vulnerable discussions about our past, the current struggles we were facing, how work and ministry were going (we solved all the problems the church was having), and relationships.

At some point, Bertucci's became a difficult place to meet for these more in-depth discussions because so many of the staff went there and people from the church that knew us. So we did what any man would do—we went to McDonald's for ice cream cones and fries in the afternoons.

We progressed through the eight stages of relationship, and trust became easy for us. Our wives often joked that we had a "bromance," but they knew that we had developed a healthy friendship where we were vulnerable with one another. We could shoot straight with each other, be accountable to each other, share our real thoughts without fear of judgment or gossip to others, and support each other through what came to be pivotal moments in our lives.

We still catch up every couple of months, as we have moved to separate parts of the country. I know that Gavin is praying for me, and when we do talk, it is like time has not passed. I believe that our vulnerability was the key to growing our relationship, solidifying it for life.

In addition to the art of vulnerability, there are other critical lessons I learned about relationships because of this friendship with Gavin. These lessons have shaped the way I see myself, how I do ministry, and how to cultivate a one-of-a-kind friendship.

1. Be yourself.

During my time in the ministry where Gavin and I worked, I had begun the process of genuinely overcoming insecurity. Gavin became one of the great encouragers in my life. Our mutual respect for each other was a catalyst for me to honestly be myself and to become more confident in sharing my thoughts and opinions without anxiety for how others will view me.

His desire and respect for my opinion were incredibly encouraging to me personally. I took that very seriously. On the flip side, I desired and respected his opinion as well. This created a mutual trust and understanding. When we talked, we didn't need to repeat phrases like, "please keep this between us," or "if someone found out about what I am sharing." My thoughts, as raw as they were, could all be on the table. Our discussions were a no-judgment zone. We could truly be ourselves, vent, share our concerns, our histories, and even our fears.

As a result, I decided to be myself in meetings, in the office, and with others where I may have struggled with other personalities. Accepting the fact that I could not and would never please everyone, I began to share my thoughts and opinions during executive team meetings, making decisions quicker (and accepting when I made a mistake), and working toward not over-analyzing how someone may have responded to me.

In the past, I would have literally lost sleep worrying about how I could "keep the peace" relationally. Gavin helped me see that "making peace" is so much more important than "keeping the peace." Some responded very well to this change in my behavior, and others criticized me as I began to challenge areas where I had the authority to speak into.

Gavin taught me the value of being myself (flaws and all), embracing the areas where I am strong while being willing to work on my weaknesses. I am so glad for these lessons.

2. Color does and doesn't matter.

I am a middle-aged white male. I was born a white male, and that will never change. On the outside, I can be identified by the color of my skin, but I refuse to be labeled and lumped into a certain mindset.

Gavin is a younger black male. He was born this way, and that will never change. On the outside, he can be identified by the color of his skin, but he refuses to be labeled and lumped into a certain mindset.

In my relationship with Gavin, I learned that color does *and* doesn't matter. It matters because it is a reality that cannot and will not change. It matters because, for me to truly have a meaningful friendship with someone of different skin color, I need to do my best to learn how the other person sees the world, or how others may see them. The trouble is that it can be different even among people who have the same skin color!

Our experiences, where we were raised, how we were raised, and what we have struggled with have shaped who we are. How we respond to it all and whether or not we are willing to learn from another's perspective will determine how we decide to embrace those who "look" different than us.

Color doesn't matter when it comes to the soul of who we are. We have all gone through great and difficult moments in relationship. Each of us has a different history. Not *one* of us has gone through the same exact experiences with the same exact perspective. We are *all* unique when it comes to our past and our present. Sure, we may all go through a similar external situation, but how we perceive and interpret this situation will be different with each person.

It can be difficult to see the world through the lens of someone else, especially with a different skin color, but color doesn't matter when it comes to sin, eternity, and our need for Jesus. I will not pretend that I "know" or "understand" what it is like for a black man to walk through life experiences. Therefore, I ask. I listen. It is imperative that we ask questions and listen, truly listen, to the answers. When we cut through the weeds of our own perspective to hear and see what someone of a different color shares about their experiences and perspective, then we can begin to comprehend how they view the room around them. We cannot and should not assume we all see things the same way.

Learning about Gavin's perspective, especially in certain situations where color is involved, has enhanced my perspective, my life, and also my relationships. Why? The reason is simple. It is because I can focus on others, begin to anticipate how my actions may affect another (whether positively or negatively), and adjust my behavior out of respect and dignity for another man's viewpoint. Another invaluable lesson.

3. We all need to laugh.

Laughter is wonderful medicine! Have you ever been in a room with someone who is laughing and cannot stop? Inevitably I will begin to chuckle and soon laugh *because* they are laughing.

Gavin's laugh is contagious. He also liked to have fun. He has a way of pointing out the humor in what others may see as a serious situation. He could turn your frown into a smile. When you are in a room with him, he quickly becomes the one we would call "the life of the party."

Many times, when we were in a serious meeting, I would get a buzz on my phone—a text message from Gavin with a funny comment that instantly made me chuckle under my breath. That led to a text string that would lighten our moods and help us to realize that stressing about what was happening in the meeting would not do us any good at all.

Laughing at yourself and not taking yourself too seriously is an art form. It frees you to be who you really are, own your weaknesses, and enjoy your strengths without becoming arrogant. Gavin is the one who taught me that.

I can remember one night in particular. All of the pastors (and their spouses if they were married) went to The Antrim House in Taneytown, MD. It was a very nice five-course meal, very fancy. My wife and I spent most of our time with Gavin and Shekinah, his wife. We must have laughed all the way home from that dinner! I laughed so hard my cheeks hurt. We laughed about things that were said at dinner, the silly little nuances we all have, and even about some of the issues we faced at the office in ministry.

There are few things Gavin does not find laughter in. His friendship has taught me to look at the lighter side of the relational equation—to have fun along the way, and to laugh...very hard.

4. Stay focused on your passions in ministry.

In ministry, it is easy to become someone you are not to be on staff at a church. However, it is essential to remember the things you are passionate about in ministry. These "things" center around our desire to serve people, counsel people, speak to and teach people, pray for people, and help people understand what it means to love God, to love others, and to be loved.

We all have a job to do, but it doesn't need to define who we are. My passion for the ministry and my life's mission is to help people understand how to love others as they love themselves—the second greatest commandment Jesus pointed out to us in Matthew 22:39. This *does* define me.

The responsibility of ministry is not to see how many people we can get to a service or how many people we can fit into a room. The burden of ministry is to use the talents, abilities, and passions in our lives to influence people toward the two greatest desires God has for us...to love Him and others as we love ourselves.

Gavin is an example to me in this because he spends his time loving people. Yes, he has a position in the church, but he is staying focused on fulfilling the desires he has to lead people of all ages to understand who God is, what a relationship with God will do for them, and how to exemplify that relationship with those around them. He stays focused on what he is passionate about.

5. Never quit learning.

Gavin has an insatiable desire to learn. He reads books, listens to speakers, seeks out wise counsel, and asks questions. He does not portray an attitude that he knows more than someone else or has learned all he needs to learn. He is vulnerable with others in a way that shows them that he is also on this journey of life. He may be further along on the journey with understanding, but he doesn't lord it over others; instead, he brings them along and helps to guide them. To learn how to navigate some of life's difficult pathways, he looks to those who may be further down that journey of faith and calls ahead to ask them for counsel.

He has shown me in his life that we are always learning. Once we stop learning, we have died. We will never fully "arrive" at complete knowledge, understanding, or full capacity. And it is through relationships that we learn and grow the fastest.

If we are not vulnerable, it portrays to others that we don't need them, when in fact we need them more than we know. This kind of friendship, like the one I have with Gavin, is not something that just comes into your life. You must recognize it, cultivate it, nurture it, invest in it, monitor it, pray for it, maintain it, and grow it. If you do, it has the potential to change the course of your life and relationships for the better.

II

The Art of Unity

"I pray that they will all be one, just as you and I are one—as you are in me, Father, and I am in you. And may they be in us so that the world will believe you sent me"
~ Jesus, John 17:21

I begin this chapter with two stories that exemplify the art of unity. Both took place while I was pastoring a "church re-plant" in Los Angeles.

DIFFERENT DAYS TO WORSHIP — STILL THE SAME GOD

I like reaching out to other pastors across denominations and the cultural lines we draw. I usually do this no matter where I live and minister, because I understand that we can accomplish far more together than we can alone in the ministry.

The first pastor to respond happened to be a Messianic Jewish pastor. This pastor and his congregation are Jewish by heritage but believe whole-heartedly believe that Jesus *is* the Messiah and their promised savior. He and I developed a connection and mutual bond through Jesus. The coolest part was that his church met on Saturdays and our church met on Sundays, so it seemed a likely next step to invite each other and our respective congregations to worship together.

At that time, I had been teaching and modeling for the church the amazing concept of unity—that we are not alone in God's Kingdom, as there are many other believers in Jesus and many different denominations of believers—our common bond is in the life, death, and resurrection of Jesus. My point was to help them understand that all other issues we raise with other believers have no bearing on eternity and where we will spend it.

We planned one weekend for our church to visit his church, sit among his attendees, worship in their style and expression, and have lunch together to develop a connection. We would be spending eternity together at some point, so why not start now?

We extended the same courtesy of relationship, inviting their church to come and worship with us. It wasn't supposed to be something we did on a regular basis but more of a learning exercise. The outcome was incredible; our eyes were opened to a different expression of love toward God—one church followed a liturgy, and the other (even though planned) followed a free-form schedule; one pastor wore a robe, and the other wore jeans and a button-down shirt; one congregation wore business casual, and the other casual comfortable. But we all worshipped Jesus Christ for all that he is.

There was no fear that people from either church were going to leave and become a part of the other. And there was no fear that we would get into lengthy disagreements on doctrine or arguments over which style of worship was better. It was an eye-opening experience for some of the leaders on my team, to say the least.

Different Ethnicities—Still the Same Creator

It was a few weeks before Easter, the celebration of Jesus' resurrection. A group of us pastors who met on a monthly basis included one pastor of a church called Successful Christian Fellowship, which was located in a community that very closely represented the ethnicity in their church—mostly African American. The church I pastored was also an even representation of the community we were serving, which was about fifty percent Caucasian, thirty percent Spanish, and the rest African American and various other ethnicities.

In building the relationship with the pastor there, our church leadership felt very strongly about having a joint service with their church at our location. The plan was to have everyone sit next to someone from the other church, worship together as we sang, take a joint offering, of which, we would split between the two churches, I would preach, and at the end of the service, our leadership team would wash the feet of their leadership team.[7]

What happened at that service was one of the most powerful connections in relationship I have experienced. Some might think this was a cheesy attempt to show reconciliation and integration. But those who might think this had to experience the humility that was evident by both sides during that ceremony to understand what had taken place. It accomplished a lasting impression and change in perspective for everyone in our churches about unity in relationship that Jesus intended from the very beginning.

After that, our church was invited to participate in a joint Good Friday service with five or six other churches. I was asked to speak on one of the

Stations of the Cross. I was the only white pastor who spoke that night. It was an honor and more than a privilege to have been invited, accepted, and embraced in relationship by these churches.

The message I spoke that day was entitled, "Pride Separates, Jesus Integrates." Using Colossians 3:1–17, I explained that pride is what truly separates us all from God and also from lasting and meaningful relationships with others. Verses 13–17 tell us to *bear with each other*—endure through, go through life with, support, sustain, uphold each other. *Forgive whatever grievances you may have against one another. Forgive as God forgave you.* You didn't earn God's forgiveness; He offered it with *no strings attached!* We are to do the same for others. These are all instructions about getting along with each other in *unity.*

Most of us desire peace in the world and harmony between all people. But even though we talk about harmony in the world and getting along with each other, it seems that unity is more of an ideal than a reality. Let's unpack this further.

The Culture of Me

What we have in society today is a "Culture-of-Me" mindset. You can see it all over the place. Whatever makes it more convenient for me will most likely get my attention. I don't have to be the one to tell you that our culture is very disunified.

The word *unity* literally means "quality of one or condition of one." Unity *is defined as oneness, sameness, or agreement.* In John 13:34–35, Jesus said to his disciples, "So now I am giving you a new commandment: Love each other. Just as I have loved you, you should love each other. Your love for one another will prove to the world that you are my disciples."

He also gave this command to his disciples and actually falls right in line with what I like to call the "True Lord's Prayer" found in John 17:20–24,

> "I am praying not only for these disciples but also for all who will ever believe in me through their message. I pray that they will all be one, just as you and I are one—as you are in me, Father, and I am in you. And may they be in us so that the world will believe you sent me. I have given them the glory you gave me, so they may be one as we are one. I am in them and you are in me. May they experience such perfect unity that the world will know that you sent me and that you love them as much as you love me."

This is what Jesus prayed over his disciples and also over us. (Note where Jesus said, "I am praying...also *for all who will ever believe in me through their message.*")

There is an excellent example of the unity I believe God desires for His children to have with each other found in Acts 4:32–35. It says:

> "All the believers were united in heart and mind. And they felt that what they owned was not their own, so they shared everything they had. The apostles testified powerfully to the resurrection of the Lord Jesus, and God's great blessing was upon them all. There were no needy people among them, because those who owned land or houses would sell them and bring the money to the apostles to give to those in need."

Walking in unity as believers does not mean we all move to a commune or compound in Texas and survive until Jesus comes back. *Unity means loving your neighbor as you love yourself.*

There are three critical thoughts about unity that can assist us in our community. This practical list comes straight out of Scripture; the principles can be applied to other areas of your life as well.

1. Unity is relational.

"Since you have been raised to new life with Christ, set your sights on the realities of heaven, where Christ sits in the place of honor at God's right hand. Think about the things of heaven, not the things of earth. For you died to this life, and your real life is hidden with Christ in God. And when Christ, who is your life, is revealed to the whole world, you will share in all his glory." (Col. 3:1–4)

This passage encourages us to set our hearts and minds on things above, where Jesus is. Unity begins with the gospel message, the message of hope that inspires us to get our relationship with God in the right place. Once we have our hearts and minds set on things above, we can then focus on the relationships we have with others here on earth. Notice how this refers us back to the two greatest commandments.

We cannot live this life without engaging in relationships with others. We are continually being relational at home, at work, with friends, with clients, with customers, the checker at the grocery store, the teller at the bank, and also at the church. Every aspect of our lives is relational with others!

Our lives are expressed in two ways: We have *time*, and we have *abilities* (talents). All of us have twenty-four hours in a day and seven days a week; how we spend that time is very important.

Let's first understand a little about time. Time is what we call a "valuable commodity." Psychologists bill by the hour. Their hours are limited and must be bought to spend that time with them. People are paid by the hour. Someone buys your time so that you will do a job.

Time is something we *all* say we wish we had more of. One of the things we need to understand is that just like money, our time needs to be *budgeted* in order of *priority*. You need time to develop relationships with people. Jesus places our relational time as number one and two on the priority list—first, time to build our relationship with God takes precedence; second, time invested in our relationships with others follows.

Our abilities or talents are things we *love* to do, things we feel *born* to do, such as speaking, writing, music, photography, humor, and creativity. We often take them for granted in our own lives, but we can incorporate these abilities or talents to develop our relationships with others and to promote unity.

We have two choices to spend our time:

- Invest our time and ability in others by providing light to the world for Jesus, by making a difference in our relationships with others, or by making a real impact in a cause or ministry.

Or, we can:

- Reserve our time and abilities for ourselves, for our own enjoyment, to build ourselves up.

When you place your mind on things above—on God, Jesus, and the power of the Holy Spirit—you will spend less time sulking over what you didn't get, and more time trying to think of ways to help others get what they need.

Many people who are *not* believers have a view on Christians where they think the phrase "Christian humor" is an oxymoron. Christians are looked at as terminally serious people, a bunch of hypocrites who tell the world what to do and how to live their lives then judge them if they don't. They see the body of Christ having difficulty getting along with each other—the *disunity*—and, therefore, miss the good witness that only comes through *unity*.

There are many people we come into contact with, and all they really want to hear is, "Your life has a purpose. God has a plan for you. Let me help you find out what it is. Don't give up!" Many hurting people don't believe they matter and they need us to put a hand on their shoulder and say a prayer for them. They need our time and our ability to listen and care for them. It doesn't take much to encourage someone else; taking the time to do it is what matters.

2. Unity is self-sacrificing.

Becoming a disciple of Christ means you must deny yourself. In Matthew 16:24, Jesus said to his disciples, "If any of you wants to be my follower, you must turn from your selfish ways, take up your cross, and follow me."

What separates us from a relationship with God? The easy answer is *sin*. What separates us from a relationship with each other? Again, the easy answer is *sin*. James 1:14–15 tell us, "Temptation comes from our own desires, which entice us and drag us away. These desires give birth to sinful actions. And when sin is allowed to grow, it gives birth to death."

So sin cannot happen unless you desire it. Sin in its very nature is found in *pride* and *selfishness*. Sin is conceived from temptation, which entices us through the evil desires of the flesh. Our sinful *desires* ("give me what I want") plus *temptation* give birth to *sin*.

Our desires say, *"Feed me. Give me what I want."* They are self-seeking and prideful. Pride and selfishness are what separates us from God and others. Philippians 2:3–4 says, "Don't be selfish; don't try to impress others. Be humble, thinking of others as better than yourselves. Don't look out only for your own interests, but take an interest in others, too." Colossians 3:10 says, "Put on your new nature, and be renewed as you learn to know your Creator and become like him."

Romans 12:3 also instructs us, "Don't think you are better than you really are. Be honest in your evaluation of yourselves, measuring yourselves by the faith God has given us." Pride and selfishness separate, but imitating Jesus and his self-sacrificing love for others integrates. The enemy has fought for dissensions, divisions, disagreements, debates, dislikes, distastes, and disdain. But Jesus desires unity. To walk in unity with other people, we must say *no* to our selfish desires and exhibit a self-sacrificing attitude.

3. Unity takes discipline.

I learned this lesson of discipline from Joe Taybron.

When my family moved to Northern California in 2013, I literally knew *no one*. I had no connections in the area (that I knew of) and had to start building relationships from scratch. My only desire was to befriend pastors, get to know them, provide a listening ear, be someone they could talk to who understood what they were going through, be a confidential confidant, and offer myself as a resource to go to if they needed anything.

I spent months and months calling churches, trying to set up coffee or lunch appointments, hoping to get some face time with the pastors in my area. It was *amazing* to me the number of pastors that wouldn't even give me an email back, or a call from their assistant, or even an inkling they had seen my name cross their desk. It was convicting because I know in the past when I pastored a church that I prioritized my time with family first, then the relationships in the church. Any relationships outside the church came last.

I'm sure I have blown off a few people in my past as well. However, as I have moved forward in ministry, I know that even just responding and letting someone know you saw them, heard them, and validated their existence can go a long way. I didn't need to meet with everyone, but I did need to acknowledge those who approached me. It was a simple matter of "Do to others whatever you would like them to do to you" (Matt. 7:12).

One pastor who accepted my invitation to meet was Joe Taybron. He had recently taken over a church in the area and was working toward his credentials in ministry. Admittedly, he was hesitant when he first took my appointment because his first thought was, "What does this guy want from me?" However, he took a step toward me, and because he values relationship, gave me an opportunity to sit down with him and exchange faith journeys. Over the last few years, we have developed a friendship where candidness, openness, dignity, integrity, honesty, and trust have bound us together.

We were at lunch one day, and he asked me a question. It was a question no one had ever really asked me before. He asked, "Why do you do *this?*" He was referring to building relationships with someone who looks different than me, was raised differently than me, and, by all appearances, was different than me.

I truly believe at that moment that my response was supernatural because in my own words I found the reason why I love building relationship with others, *"Because the differences that we have are not as important as the relationship that we can enjoy."*

My calling in life was confirmed once again. I was born to build relationships.

Jesus said, "Love your neighbor as yourself," (Mark12:31), and "so that they may be brought to complete unity. Then the world will know that you sent me and have loved them even as you have loved me," (John 17:23, NIV). Since he uttered these words, the enemy has been hard at work to separate us by any means necessary. In reality, Satan has been trying to separate us from God and each other since the creation of the world.

The level of distrust and competition between churches in the same city is beyond comprehension. It becomes so comfortable to avoid the confrontation of interpreting Scripture. We retreat into a cocoon of a denomination (or church, or non-denomination). We have made Scripture the catalyst for division when it should be the very thing that should unite us.

Relationships are messy.

With anything that takes effort, *discipline* (work) is needed to maintain a spirit of unity in relationships. It is one thing to discuss the need for unity; it is another actually to put it into practice.

Discipline requires one to become a disciple of Jesus first. We see this in Colossians 3:9–11, where Paul says,

> "Don't lie to each other, for you have stripped off your old sinful nature and all its wicked deeds. Put on your new nature, and be renewed as you learn to know your Creator and become like him. In this new life, it doesn't matter if you are a Jew or a Gentile, circumcised or uncircumcised, barbaric, uncivilized, slave, or free. Christ is all that matters, and he lives in all of us."

Even in the days when Paul wrote to this church in Colossae, people were divided. They were separated by casts, socioeconomic status, ethnicity, beliefs, and preferences. Some were even teaching that to believe in Jesus, you *must* be circumcised. Paul blasts that belief into oblivion by stating, very simply, that the sections we have divided ourselves into are of no circumstance in the eyes of God.

This way of thinking was and is so different than how we continue to live our lives, even today. We are still so separated. I would not expect those who do not know Jesus to be forced to adapt to this line of thinking. I would, however, expect those who believe in Jesus and live for Him to understand and live in such a way with other believers that shows we are in complete unity with each other, if not for the express purpose of living out the prayer Jesus prayed in John 17:20–23,

> "My prayer is not for them alone. I also pray for those who believe in me through their message, that ALL of them may be one, Father, just as you are in me and I am in you. May they also be in us so that the world may believe that you have sent me. I have given them the glory that you gave me, that they may be one as we are one: I in them and you in me. May they be brought to complete unity to let the world know that you sent me and have loved them even as you have loved me."

Renewing Our Minds

In Romans 12:2, Paul calls for us to renew our minds. He says,

"Don't copy the behavior and customs of this world, but let God transform you into a new person by changing the way you think. Then you will learn to know God's will for you, which is good and pleasing and perfect."

Renewing our minds is a learning process. A disciple is one who learns. In life, you should never stop learning. Once you stop learning, you cease to live. The more you learn about God, the more your mind will become renewed. You cannot learn more about God and stay the same. Learning about God means you will be changed for the better. Makes sense, doesn't it?

When you discipline yourself to practice what you learn, you will begin to see others as God sees them. In the image of the Creator, there is no Jew or Greek; no black, white, or brown; no male or female. Spiritual discipline drives us to a *deeper relationship with God.*

There are many ways to discipline ourselves to promote *unity* in relationships with those around us. Colossians 3:12–17 is a great place to start for a practical list of actions to focus on. As you practice them, you will see your attitude change toward others, as well as their attitude toward you. Let's review them.

1. Clothe ourselves with tender-hearted mercy, kindness, humility, gentleness, and patience.

2. Make allowance for each other's faults, and forgive *anyone* who offends you. (See also Matt. 6:14–15)

3. Most importantly, clothe ourselves with love, which binds us all together in perfect harmony (unity).

4. Let the peace of Christ rule our hearts.

5. As members of one body, we are called to live in peace with each other.

6. Always be thankful.

7. Let the message about Christ fill our lives; in other words, let our speech signal others that we are followers of Jesus.

8. Teach and counsel each other with all the wisdom he gives. (See also Prov. 27:17)

9. Sing psalms, hymns, and spiritual songs to God with thankful hearts (express your love openly).

10. And finally, whatever you do or say, remember you are representing Jesus, and in so doing, you are offering thanks through Jesus to God the Father.

All of these practical instructions can be exercised in our lives and should be evident in our core principles. We develop bonds as believers to worship, growing, and serving one another in the context of relationships. Our relationships are places where disciples of Jesus can love their neighbor as themselves and walk in unity with their fellow believers. This is a community where faith comes alive.

PART TWO

Obstacles of Relationship

12.

Overcoming Inhibition and Insecurity

Inhibitions—those pesky little thoughts that keep us from doing something, accomplishing something, speaking to someone, taking a risk, seizing that moment, speaking in front of a group of people, getting on a roller coaster, flying down a zip line, stepping onto stage...the list goes on and on. We allow these thoughts to influence us in such a way that they stop us from entering into, developing, or even taking the time to be in "relationship" with others.

Insecurities is another word for inhibitions. You can tell when they crop up by the words that come into our thought-streams: "I can't...," "I don't...," "no one will...," or "who are you to...?" When they do, we have a choice to make. Do we allow those thoughts to cripple us, keeping us on the ledge that foregoes relationships with others? Or will we jump off that ledge into the waters below, immersing ourselves into the messiness of relationships?

I had become quite proficient at hiding my insecurities. I remember one evening while volunteering for childcare, I spent a few hours speaking to a new friend that had only been an acquaintance before that night. It was eye-opening to hear that she thought I was unapproachable because I didn't speak much to anyone when they walked by. I told her it was because I thought they would not notice or talk to me. After that night, I decided to change my perspective on others. My inhibitions and insecurities had driven me to judge others before getting to know them without giving them a chance to share their story. This caused me to miss out on some great friendships.

That wasn't okay with me anymore.

It was Bible college during my senior year when my insecurities really rose to the surface. One of my classes centered around expository preaching and the end-of-term project was to write and preach a sermon in front of the class. The instructor and class were to choose two of those sermons to be given in front of the entire college during a Friday chapel service (the most well-attended chapel of the week). Those in attendance would not only be the students, but the whole faculty, admin staff, the president of the college, and pastors from the area would be there too.

Needless to say, I thought I would never be chosen.

However, my professor and the students in the class saw something in me that I had heard when I was younger but had long since suppressed. The first time I spoke in front of a group of people to teach, I was eighteen years old. My uncle allowed me to teach on a Wednesday night. Several people came up to me afterward and said there was something about my speaking that made them want to listen. They wanted to listen!

I was chosen as one of the two senior speakers elected out of the entire class to give the Friday chapel sermon. I could not get out of this one. It was one of the most challenging assignments I had ever done, but it also resulted in a breakthrough. The insecurities of losing face with the entire school if I did not speak well were overridden by the insecurities of what they would think of me after I was done talking.

That sermon—spoken to over five hundred peers, professors, and pastors—began the awareness of insecurity and my journey to fight daily against the negative effects of allowing it to take over my decisions, relationships, and potential accomplishments.

Our insecurities are the inner screams we wish no one would hear. We do not want to confess them, for fear they make us look weak. When someone discovers them or sees them in us, we build up a fortress that looks strong on the outside. As a matter of fact, I can hear that inner voice right now saying, "No one wants you to write about this. What if someone thinks less of you or stops caring what you are writing?"

Yes, that's right. I have struggled with battling my inhibitions and insecurities most of my adult life. I wish I could say I have overcome them. However, whenever I get close to a success, the battle rages. I have become more proficient at silencing these thoughts, but I remain humbled by them nonetheless. Why would *anyone* confess this? I must be crazy, right?

Maybe. One thing I have learned is that being vulnerable up front (not baring all my faults, but showing others that I am who I am, faults and all) tends to shoot down the negative thoughts flying around my thought airfield. It has taken me a long time, and I am not successful at this all the time. Yet, when I am faced with the uncertainty, anxiety, and diffidence surrounding me, it has become easier to climb over those emotional obstacles when I make the decision *not* to listen to them.

360° Work Review

The process of being able to overcome the emotional obstacle of insecurity jump-started in 2012. I was one of eight on a senior-level team that oversaw a large ministry organization. The senior leader had us perform a 360° evaluation, which dove into areas such as the culture of the workplace, character, job relationships, and competence.

Personality profiles are a fun exercise for me. I like to self-evaluate to see how I have changed or adapted to the environment, how I have grown, and what areas still need improvement. However, *this* evaluation was much different. Along with my own self-evaluation, all of my colleagues, my boss, and my closest family and friends took the same evaluation. A consultant reviewed all the responses and sat with us one-on-one to go over potential issues, how we fit into the team, wins, and the possibility of blind spots we could seek guidance for.

When it was my turn to sit down with the consultant, I discovered that most people saw me for who I was. However, all of the responses on the negative side said something like, *"There isn't really anything negative I can say about Dan that is glaring, but he could improve by ...,"* or *"He needs to show more confidence because his opinion is valued."*

Were my eyes ever opened!

What I thought I had overcome in my life, others around me at work, at home, and in friendships pointed right to the issue without being able to place their finger on exactly what the issue was. I knew exactly what the issue was and my heart sank.

They were all pointing to the deep sense of insecurity I have battled for most of my teen and adult life. This insecurity had woven its way into every aspect of my life and relationships. For the most part, it hadn't destroyed any relationships, but it certainly held me back from realizing deep and meaningful ones. I had held people at arm's length for fear of their discovering I was not as confident as I seemed outwardly. The trouble is, they all saw it.

Since that time, I have made a distinct effort to be open with this issue. With guidance, prayer, and stepping out in faith, I can daily overcome this feeling of insecurity and move forward with confidence.

Do I still fail? Do I still make mistakes? Yes! When I do fail, do I still battle with the afterthoughts that try to plague my next step forward? You betcha! The difference, you might ask? I embrace it now. Sometimes I need a good swift kick in the aft deck by someone that loves me to remind me that I am slipping into the lake of timidity—"*Just cut it out! Pick yourself up off the mat and go back swinging!*"

Kobe Bryant, point guard for the L.A. Lakers, said, "I have self-doubt. I have insecurity. I have fear of failure. I have nights when I show up at the arena and I'm like, 'My back hurts, my knees hurt. I don't have it. I just want to chill.' We all have self-doubt. You don't deny it, but you also don't capitulate to it. You embrace it."[8]

As we age, one would think these insecurities fall away. But the insecurities we have while we are younger may actually become even more intense. They can be elevated to doubting whether someone sees value in us anymore because we are older and we feel irrelevant. It is so important as we age to continue to develop relationships that will encourage and counsel us. Relationships don't just have to be with people our own age. In fact, I encourage everyone to intentionally make relationships with people who look up to us in *our* age and become a mentor to them or simply befriend them.

Our insecurities are wrapped up in our own minds. If we branch out in our relationships, not only will we find out we are still useful, but we can have an even more significant impact on the coming generations.

What would happen, if today, you decided to step forward and take a risk in one of your relationships—one that says, "I don't want to pretend to be something to impress someone. I will be myself even if that means I show my faults."? I challenge you to give it a try. Find a safe environment, some people you can trust. Open up about your inhibitions and insecurities and what you feel is holding you back. Allow them to speak into your life and call you out when you allow those pesky thoughts to hold you back.

One of the single greatest obstacles in our lives that keep us from experiencing deep and meaningful relationships with each other is our insecurities, which speak to our hearts and lie to us by saying we will never be accepted if people knew of our weaknesses and failings.

Resolve today to speak to your insecurities and tell them they can no longer influence you. Then resolve tomorrow to do the same. It takes one day at a time and will become easier as you become consistent and practice this daily.

13.

Overcoming Jealousy

My dogs have always craved attention. At one time we had three—a basset hound, mini-dachshund (now passed), and a chihuahua mix (a mix with what we haven't figured out yet!). If I called one of them, all of them would come. If I started to pet one of them, the others jumped up and came over to get the attention. The dachshund, with his mini legs, propped his front paws up onto the basset. The chihuahua leaped and also propped herself onto either dog. All of them vied for the two hands I had to offer them. It was a challenge at first, but I developed a sweeping petting motion to get all three! It is very affirming to have pets bark and greet you when you come home.

The great thing about pets is they cannot talk back to you. If there is a conflict with one of them, they get scolded, and eventually, they come right back begging for your attention! Could you imagine a workplace like that? I can't either.

Dogs are pack animals. There is an alpha, and all the other dogs contend for the attention of that alpha, if even just to be considered higher in the order. In the house, my (now two) dogs consider me the alpha. If one of them is getting something from me, the other one comes over to receive it too. This is especially true if I am pulling apart a rotisserie chicken. They both sit patiently watching every move my hands make. If I raise my hand with a piece of meat in it, their heads lift up. If I toss it in the air, they compete to get it.

The chihuahua is the worst offender, but also one of the most loving creatures. She will literally push herself into the fray and place her head under my hand to get the affection over the dog. I can only give her a smile and a chuckle as I equally spread the love for both. What is it that causes this response in dogs? For that matter, what is it that causes a similar reaction in people?

When someone else receives an award...

When someone else goes on a vacation to a place we have always desired to go...

When someone else gets a promotion at work...

When one of our closest relatives makes more money...

When someone else gets the job we wanted...

When someone else buys a 70-inch television, and now our 65-inch is not good enough...

When someone else has the affections of a person we desire to be with...

In a word—*jealousy*. While this will not be a chapter teaching all about dog behavior, there is some value in trying to understand the concept of jealousy through the dogs' example. The truth is that most of us have said the words "I'm jealous of..." at some point in our lives. We become jealous when we observe someone obtain, purchase, love, own, and enjoy an object, job, relationship, or whatever it is that we would like to have. Jealousy can be very ugly and is another big obstacle that we must overcome to have meaningful and long-lasting relationships with others.

Jealousy focuses our attention on what we *do not* have and our perception of what someone else *does* have. It is very self-focused. We often see jealousy rear its ugly head in romantic relationships and it ends up tearing those relationships apart. A man or a woman becomes jealous of the object of their affection's time or any other person (or thing) capturing their attention. The problem is that it usually has the adverse effect than intended, which is that the other person would notice the jealous behavior and do whatever is needed to appease it. But actually, the object of the jealousy feels so restricted that all they desire to do is break free. The jealousy response ultimately breaks down trust between couples if it is not dealt with.

However, I must add that signs of jealousy, when handled appropriately, can actually make a relationship stronger. Let me give you an example. I tend to work...*a lot*. When I work so many hours, I am not at home. Even when I am at home, I am not "at home" in my mind. My wife sometimes gets to the point where she will not-so-subtly remind me when I am not present. I have learned to recognize when she says certain things that she has healthy jealousy of my time spent away. Adjusting my work schedule and becoming more intentional about being at home and present with my family all but erases any feelings of jealousy creeping up in our relationship.

What causes jealousy? In a phrase: wanting for ourselves what we believe someone else has. In my wife's case, her jealousy concerned more than just her—she wanted the time and attention I was spending on everything and everyone else to be spent on both her and the kids. A reasonable request that husbands and fathers would be well advised to mind.

Unhealthy jealousy, though, is entirely focused on ourselves. It is the very opposite of loving someone as yourself. The good news is that it has difficulty thriving when we become focused on meeting the needs of others. Jealousy cannot survive when we are grateful for what we do have and celebrate when others have successes. It cannot destroy our relationships if we decide to be thankful for what we have and focus our attention on those things or people. And it cannot fester if we can learn to be content with our life.

Paul, in one of his letters to the church of Philippi, alluded to his learned ability to be content with what he has, no matter the situation. Philippians 4:11–12 says,

> "Not that I was ever in need, for I have learned how to be content with whatever I have. I know how to live on almost nothing or with everything. I have learned the secret of living in every situation, whether it is with a full stomach or empty, with plenty or little."

Our attitudes determine the path we will take. A jealous attitude can send us down a dangerous path of relational destruction when we start to believe we *deserve* something. It can tempt us to do things dishonestly, to spend more than we have, to pass blame when the blame belongs to you, to put others down to lift ourselves up, and also to enter into a self-deprecating perspective that becomes a vicious cycle of "woe is me."

But imagine what would happen in our own lives and attitude towards others when we share in the joys of another person's achievements; when we show them honor and are dignified in our relationships; and when we trust God with our level of contentment as He takes care of our needs. What would it look like in this world if we were all more aware of the needs of others around us? What kind of society would we live in if the goal were to give, rather than to receive? I know the answer: our world and relationships would be better, happier, and more peaceful.

So how can you combat jealousy? Pay attention to your thoughts. When jealousy begins to creep into your thinking or your heart, recognize the self-induced emotion that wants something someone else has. Take that thought or feeling and transform it into an act of love and humility. This is hard to do, but commit to it, and I guarantee you will see your relationships with others enhance.

It is natural to think of ourselves first. However, there is an instruction in Romans 12:15 to "be happy with those who are happy, and weep with those who weep." This points our attention to the other person. When they are happy about something, we can rejoice with them. When they are mourning a loss, we mourn with them.

Becoming others-focused will propel us forward in healthy relationships. We can check our motives and humble ourselves, choosing to not give weight to what others have that we do not. If we do need something, like our spouse's time and attention, we can resist acting out of jealousy and instead communicate our need in a healthy way. When our motives become others-focused, and we begin to allow humility to permeate our thoughts and actions, then our desire to help others will come through. Humility is the antidote to jealousy. Jealousy cannot reside where humility has moved in.

14.

Overcoming Unhealthy Relationships

When I was very young, I can remember so vividly my mother and father urging me to make good choices with kids I hung out with. But there was a time in second grade, the years when a young boy wants to be accepted by his friends when I got myself into quite a spot. During lunch, a couple of boys in my class were hatching a plan to keep our sandwich bags and ask the teacher to excuse us to go to the bathroom, at different times of course. They planned to fill up our sandwich bags with water and have a water balloon fight.

Who does that? Seven-year-old boys do, that's who.

It was a full-proof plan until someone decided to stuff their bag down the sink drain and the water began to back up and flooded the bathroom. We all tried to stop the water from flowing, and we tried to clean up the floor with paper towels, but they just stopped up the floor drain even more. It was a circus of craziness.

Then it happened. The teacher knocked on the door and announced she was coming in. One of the boys ran into the stall and acted like he wasn't part of the sandwich-bag mayhem. Another boy tried to run out the door. And two of us were left standing over the drain and sink with a dazed look on our faces.

Needless to say, we were all sent to the principal's office. It was one of the scariest fifteen minutes of my life. There I sat, waiting for the principal to come in, with wet pant legs and soggy shoes and socks, evidence that I had been part of the debacle. Guilty.

My mom was called. When she arrived, I don't remember much of the conversation. But what I do remember is what happened when I got home. I was disciplined. I was also told, once again, that who I decide to hang out with determines who I choose to become. She commanded me to stay away from the boys who influenced me to do this deed.

Being from a Christian family, I was also given the Bible verses to remind me that sometimes we need to disconnect from unhealthy relationships to keep our life on the right path. Verses like:

> "Bad company corrupts good character." (1 Cor. 15:33)

> "Walk with the wise and become wise; associate with fools and get in trouble." (Prov. 13:20)

> "Stay away from fools, for you won't find knowledge on their lips." (Prov. 14:7)

That day is etched in my memory. I wish I could say I always stayed away from doing stupid things after that day, but there were many tempting times when I allowed others to influence me, which when mixed with my desire to be accepted, equated into making dumb mistakes and getting in trouble.

You could say that my unhealthy relationships created obstacles for me to live a healthy life. Sometimes we just need to disconnect from them, perhaps for a long or short time, or even permanently. But how can we know which degree of disconnection is warranted? It starts with acknowledging and accepting the reasons *why* we need connection with others in the first place, and what kinds of relationships we *should* be connected to. We need to know what healthy relationships look like.

If you remember from chapter two, there are four reasons to connect with other people:

1. *It benefits me.* In a mutual relationship, it just makes sense that it would be beneficial to me personally. Otherwise, why would I even want to connect? Even if I am helping someone and it seems one-sided, I benefit from the feeling I get when I do it.

2. *It benefits you.* In a mutual relationship, I must be concerned with your well-being. Even if I am the recipient of what you can provide, in return you would benefit from the feeling you get when you do something for me.

3. *It should benefit others.* If working properly, our mutual relationship should eventually have positive consequences for others around us. With mutual respect and dignity for each other, we see the value in others and do what we can to help them, especially because of what we have experienced together.

4. *It pleases God.* To love your neighbor as you love yourself is not only the second greatest commandment Jesus gave us but the purpose of why we were created.

So anyone who meets these criteria is someone you should consider forming a relationship with. Keep in mind that not *all* connections turn into or *should* turn into long-term relationships. Some are better off as acquaintances.

There is one relationship that is first and foremost, however, that serves as a gauge for how good a relationship is for us—our personal relationship with Jesus Christ. Jesus has a way of illuminating the darkness if we tune into it.

"I have come as a light to shine in this dark world, so that all who put their trust in me will no longer remain in the dark." (John 12:46)

It is possible that we may need to move away from a relationship with someone because they negatively influence us from having a good connection with God. If we continually put ourselves into places where God is not celebrated or where our relationship with Him is compromised, we will eventually, sooner than later, begin to feel as if God is distant and our connection with Him lost. Why is this important? Because connection with God pleases Him—we were made for relationship with Him and others, remember? Our relationships with others will be so much more enhanced the more we directly connect to God in relationship.

Connecting with God is simply to get alone with Him and connect directly to Him. God tells us to, "Be still and know that I am God" (Ps. 46:10). So when you feel like the closest relationships in your life are in jeopardy, or you are moving at a hundred miles an hour, and you cannot keep up the pace, find a moment to rest your mind, body, and heart. You can be still before God and be reminded of who He is, what He has done, and where He has taken you. He can give you a new and fresh perspective about the health, or unhealthiness, of your relationships.

Often, all we need to do is stop for just a moment in time and look up. Like a dog, who walks next to his master looks back to keep a frame of reference, we ought to keep our focus on where God is at all times too. The best part is, He is always just beside us. We don't need to look far.

You can find true rest in your spirit and innermost being by being in His presence. When we live with Jesus as our shelter—our covering—we know our relationships with others, even if thrown into tumult, can be restored and reconciled. Getting alone with God is the best antidote, the best course-correction, to reboot and replenish the relationships around us.

Sometimes, disconnection means we just need a break from people—we need to disconnect with them temporarily to refocus. Jesus did this, so why would we think we are *not* in need of it?

"After sending them home, he went up into the hills by himself to pray. Very early in the morning, while it was still dark, Jesus got up, left the house and went off to a solitary place, where he prayed." (Matt. 14:23)

If Jesus needed to break away from people, the very reason he was here on this earth to begin with, we certainly need to as well. The primary relationship in our lives is and should be our relationship with God. We were created to be in a relationship with Him first. So when we don't spend time with God in relationship, we become incredibly vulnerable to all of the behaviors and actions that are opposite of who God is and what He wants to do in our lives. Time with Him means an abundance of joy. No time with Him and we may fill our minds with thoughts that are counter-productive to a balanced life in relationship with Him and others.

Have a daily time with God, where you break away from everyone around you. Get alone with Him and allow Him to speak to you through His Word, as the Holy Spirit reminds you of all the things that Jesus taught.

"You must love the Lord your God with all your heart, all your soul, and all your mind." (Matt. 22:37)

It is possible to get ourselves into situations where we place obstacles between Him and us, thus making it easier to put obstacles between us and others. An obstacle between God and me is anything that gets in the way of my relationship with Him. That could include certain people, activities, or even responsibilities. He can guide us in who and what they are.

We want to make sure to find a community of people where we are consistently hearing about and experiencing a close connection to God. This can be in a small group at church, a Bible study at home, or even making sure we go to church and other functions where the distractions of life will not pull us away. These will lead to healthy relationships.

Also, it is so important to keep yourself charged with God's Spirit and stay connected to Him. This is true for strength in our daily lives and for our relationships with others to stay on track. For me, it involves taking time every morning to read the Bible, read a devotional book, writing down three things I am grateful for, and writing out my prayer for the day. At night, I take some time to process the day and write down how it went, thanking God for another day to live. What does it look like for you?

Our relationship with God should be first and foremost the *most important* relationship in our life. God never moves. His strength is sustaining, and His love for us is always there. When you begin to feel distant from God, remember the love you had for Him when you first accepted Him as your Source, your life, and the only One that can bring you into that relationship. He is our strength, our peace, and our hope.

When we stray from this relationship with God and choose not to focus on it, the weaker our connection to Him. Notice when I said "when we stray"; God never strays from us. There have been times in my life where I did not do a daily devotion, did not pray for days at a time, and just came home, turned on the television, and vegged out. Over time, I found myself asking where God was and if He heard me when I prayed. I had strayed from my relationship with Him. Do this for a day or two, and you know it. Do this for a month, and everyone close to you knows it. Do it for a year, and everyone can see it.

THE LURE OF UNHEALTHY RELATIONSHIPS

Hopefully, now we can better discern if there are unhealthy relationships that we may need to disconnect from. This is easier said than done! What is it that draws us toward unhealthy relationships?

This question has baffled me for many years. I now know that I choose the relationships in my life that I will invest in and which ones I need to let go of. As I get older, I realize that I don't have time to battle with unhealthy relationships.

Growing up and in college, the draw for many of us is to be accepted. If we become desperate enough, we can compromise our own convictions to *feel* accepted. Fear of rejection becomes one of the top reasons, in my opinion, for why we are drawn to unhealthy relationships.

We can also be enticed to enter into unhealthy relationships when we want to do something that makes us feel good, and we willingly push aside our convictions to get that feeling. We allow our emotions to drive our decisions in life and can end up neglecting our relationship with God and shy away from healthy relationships that encourage us toward healthy living.

Some of us grew up around dysfunction and abuse; it's all we know. This actually may require some professional help through a counselor or therapist who draws from the Bible for wisdom to determine who or what is holding us back. Others of us are drawn away by sinful actions that we choose to be a part of, knowing they negatively affect our relationship with God and the healthy relationships in our lives.

All of us at some point, or even now, have made a choice or are making a decision, allowing negative, unhealthy relationships to influence us. It is what we do about it that matters.

Disconnecting from Unhealthy Relationships

We *choose* the relationships we enter into, and sometimes it becomes necessary for us to *disconnect* from relationships that are not conducive to our moving forward in a healthy way. We can *choose* to disengage from *any* relationship, at any time, and for any reason.

No one is forcing us to stay connected to unhealthy relationships. And they are not always easy to let go of, especially if we have been connected to them for any extended amount of time. Sometimes unhealthy relationships are habitual, or disconnection is very complicated, or maybe life is just too comfortable because change is hard.

Disconnecting does not have to have negative connotations. It also does not have to be permanent, although that may be necessary. It would be incredibly valuable to disconnect especially if the relationship does one or more of these three things. One is if the person or group draws us away from a focused and intentional relationship with God. When someone, or a group of someones, influences us to compromise our faith in God or our moral boundaries, it is time to disconnect. Second, the relationship has caused us to change to the point where we have become the very thing we despise in others. The Proverbs warn us of this very thing:

> "Don't befriend angry people or associate with hot-tempered people, or you will learn to be like them and endanger your soul." (Prov. 22:24–25)

> "Guard your heart above all else, for it determines the course of your life." (Prov. 4:23)

The third is if a person or group of people is taking advantage of us—we find ourselves on the giving end with no reciprocation. This is not referring to equality and mutual respect and admiration. This is when someone knows you have something they need or want, and they entertain a relationship with you only to continue benefitting from it.

Sometimes the disconnection only needs to be short to *correct* the issue, and then, if possible, reconnect through *reconciliation*. In coaching others, whether for life coaching or career coaching, I have come across several people who needed to follow the instructions to disconnect from a relationship for a short, pre-arranged time in order to regain strength, perspective, and to set aside the distraction of the relationship in order to work on what is important personally.

One person I coached had a close family relationship where it was evident there were some dysfunctional tendencies. For one thing, there were no boundaries set in place. The family member would text, call or email at all times. This person felt obligated to respond immediately and felt like they had to fix every issue that arose because of the text, call, or email. After all, this was a close relationship! This family member's actions disrupted this person's life to the point where the stress was overwhelming and put a significant strain on the relationship. No matter how this person communicated to their family member, they did not respect the boundaries they tried to set in place. My recommendation was to temporarily block the family member's phone number from calls and texts, and also to block their email address—both for two weeks.

At first, this person was very unsure if they could even go for three days. Admittedly, it was challenging. However, even if you decided to go cold turkey from caffeine or sugar, you will possibly experience headaches, shakes, and cravings for at least three to five days. When you break through the wall of the side effects, it becomes easier to focus, set boundaries, and find ways to clearly communicate those boundaries in a loving, dignified way. It also becomes easier to enforce them.

When we met two weeks later, this person was ecstatic and said, "You would be so proud of me! I was able to go the full two weeks!" The result of the two-week hiatus was an ability to set healthy boundaries, which were heard loud and clear through radio-silence. The family member now understood that the boundaries were not merely suggestions. This person broke away for a temporary time to bring reconciliation. The coachee felt like they had regained control of their time and life.

Of course, the process had not been completed, as this person still needed to go back to their family member and reconnect. Reconciliation needed to take place along with re-communicating the boundaries and rules of engagement. In the end, this person's connection to their family member became healthier and stronger.

Sometimes it is essential to disconnect when things are going poorly in the relationship, and especially when your relationship with God is suffering because of it. A ministry started by Saddleback Church called Celebrate Recovery is very proficient in helping people accomplish this disconnection. You can find these groups in your local area and visit if you feel you are surrounded by dysfunction and cannot break the cycle.

> "Walk with the wise and become wise; associate with fools and get in trouble." (Prov. 13:20)

Steps to Take for Disconnection

We have spent *a lot* of time understanding why our relationship to God and others can be damaged. The question is now how to disconnect from unhealthy relationships with people? One thing you could do is just to walk away. One of the best ways to disconnect is to tell yourself that you need to move on, and physically remove yourself from the individual(s) who has been an obstacle in your life.

Some might say, "Well, we *need* to be willing to witness and share God's love with everyone." While this is true, there is nothing that says we need to place ourselves in a compromising temptation to do so. There is an inherent incompatibility that requires disconnection. Here are some thoughts to remember when deciding to leave a relationship that we know is damaging. When we disconnect, whether temporarily or indefinitely, do so...

...with grace and truth;

Be honest with yourself and with others about your boundaries. Dr. Henry Cloud and Dr. John Townsend wrote an incredible work called *Boundaries: When to Say Yes, When to Say No—To Take Control of Your Life.* When you communicate with grace and truth, you will understand there are certain limits which you should never cross. If someone tries to force you or you get easily tempted to cross those lines, set a boundary in your life. You can do this with your friends, family, work, and any relationship. The only relationship you and I should not have boundaries with—nor can we have any boundaries with—is with God.[9]

Show dignity and separate yourself with honor for others. This is the grace part. We are taking full responsibility for our own actions. This is not a blame on someone else, because we are ultimately the reason we do what we do, say what we say, and go where we go. We can honor others by being respectful in our disconnection, not speaking poorly (slander) or microphone dropping negative comments or remarks as we disconnect. This person is still someone that God considers worthy of the life of Jesus on the cross.

...in humility;

Disconnect without turning people off from a relationship with God. We should *never* say, "God told me to disconnect with you." Why place the blame on God when we are the ones that are having the difficulty with our own boundaries? This can be difficult to do, no doubt. However, our desire should be to point people to Jesus, not turn them away from him. We can do this by squarely placing the responsibility for the disconnection where it belongs—on ourselves. This takes *humility.*

When we humble ourselves, we present to those in our lives that we are not perfect but in need of the love, forgiveness, and guidance from God. Our relationships with others are too important to *not* spend quality time with

Him. When we do build our relationship with God, we find our relationships with others is brought more into focus. We see others as "worthy" of the life of Jesus on the cross. We begin to see how humility is our friend and not a weakness. We can place all of our relationships into perspective and have discernment when one is failing, and wisdom about what to do when one needs to be nurtured.

Take some time right now. If you are inclined, place this book down, and get alone with God. Pray over your relationships and consider what God is telling you about them.

PART THREE

Building Blocks
of Relationship

15

The Art of Hope

*"A true relationship is two imperfect people refusing
to give up on each other."*
~ Anonymous

*"You can't just give up on someone because the situation's not ideal.
Great relationships aren't great because they have no problems.
They're great because both people care enough about the other
person to find a way to make it work."*
~ Anonymous

D o you have any relationships that have been damaged?

My bet? Your answer is yes.

How it became damaged probably happened one of two ways:

1. You were the cause because of something you said, did, or are currently doing;

2. Your friend, family member, or co-worker was the cause because of something they said, did, or are currently doing.

Damaged relationships hurt. They create heartbreak and pain in our lives that tend to hang on for a long time. We can respond to the pain in many ways, the first way being resentment. We can become resentful and pass the blame on to the other person, whether we were the cause of it or not *(I do not recommend this)*. Second, we can allow the hurt to affect our other relationships negatively. When we focus so much on the pain of what happened, our other relationships suffer *(also not recommended)*. Third, we can try to see our responsibility in the hurt and do our best to reconcile the relationship *(recommended!)*. Or fourth, we can understand that sometimes the other person needs to go through their own trial, that we were not the root cause of the hurt but possibly the unfortunate target. In this response, we allow time to pass and pray the other person comes around *(also recommended along with #3)*.

We just spent the entire last chapter talking about how to disconnect from unhealthy relationships. What happens if we disconnected from someone and now we want to reconcile with them? The ultimate goal is to mend our damaged relationships if we can. Sometimes it is not possible, but we can commit to hope.

Hope is a very powerful go-to response that will help us stay on the path to restoration.

It is defined as "a feeling of expectation and desire for a certain thing to happen." In this case a restored relationship. I love the quote by the Nobel Peace Prize winner Desmond Tutu, who held out a lot of hope for the end of apartheid in Southern Africa. "Hope is being able to see that there is light despite all of the darkness," he said.[10] Hope in God and His power to restore gives us that light.

Romans 5:3–4 gives us instruction about what to do during problems or trials.

> "We can rejoice, too, when we run into problems and trials, for we know that they help us develop endurance. And endurance develops strength of character, and character strengthens our confident hope of salvation."

Perseverance means refusing to give up on someone or something just because we are facing difficulty. As we persevere, our trials and problems help us develop endurance. Living out of that endurance builds strength in our character, which strengthens our faith—our hope—in Jesus' ability to save and restore us, the other person, and the relationship.

It is because of hope that relationships can be saved, revived, and restored. Without it, we can't get past hurts done against us, and we cannot expect others to get past what we've done or neglected to do for them. So then, reflecting on the Romans passage above helps us to know that hope is one of the critical building blocks of relationship, a very powerful one that does several things:

1. Hope *gives life* to a relationship—it *perseveres*. The hurt is still there, but hope helps people to say, "I'm not giving up on this friend, family member, or co-worker." It is tough to be in a relationship with someone who is brokenhearted or breaks your heart. Try and try, sometimes a friend or family member will need our perseverance to keep hope alive.

2. Hope *saves*. Someone could be swimming in a sea of despair, floating in the dark night of the soul, and then a word of

encouragement comes, and hope is ignited. That hope can be the lifeline they, or you can hold on to.

3. Hope provides a *new perspective*. It can open our eyes to see the *possibility* of a reconciled relationship, that we will be able to get closer to someone to speak life into their heart. We learn how to put into context the issues we face, and we also realize that everyone is at a different place, so sometimes we need to be patient, and other times we need others to be patient with us.

4. Hope says that relationships *can be restored despite the circumstances* that surrounded, shrouded, or confused them. I have seen marital relationships come back from unfaithfulness, pain, misunderstanding, confusion, and long-standing hurt. As long as there is breath in our lungs and a heartbeat pounding inside our chest, there is hope for a restored relationship.

Of course, reconciliation takes two people to make it happen. However, that is where prayer comes in. Prayer, simply put, is communication with God. We can talk to Him and let Him know what is going on in our relationships. Remember, first and foremost, we are to love God with all of our heart, mind, soul, and strength—to be in relationship with Him. I guarantee that He knows and can handle whatever issue you may have. Ask Him for the wisdom in how to deal with the hurt of a relationship and to help mend whatever damage was done, no matter *who* was the cause. What God can do in a heart or mind of someone is miraculous. We may not be able to reach them, but God can. Psalm 147:3 says, "He heals the brokenhearted and binds up their wounds." He can heal them and us emotionally and psychologically; He will get us through this.

As we stay close to God in relationship, He begins to open up our eyes to the hurts of others—the issues others face and the triggers our loved ones and we have. Because God helps us, if something happens between friends that hurt one or the other or both of you, it doesn't have to be the end. You can have *hope* that the relationship will mend.

Moving Towards Restoration

To restore a relationship, we know we can commit to hope and pray. But what else can we do? What is our part in the restoration process? The Scriptures tell us, "If it is possible, as far as it depends on you, live at peace with everyone" (Rom. 12:18, NIV). There are some specific things we can resolve to do that will, at least on our part, drive us closer to the destination of a healed relationship.

Resolve to reconcile.

> "All this is from God, who reconciled us to himself through Christ and gave us the ministry of reconciliation: that God was reconciling the world to himself in Christ, not counting people's sins against them. And he has committed to us the message of reconciliation." (2 Cor. 5:18–19)

Resolving to reconcile can strengthen a relationship even through the difficulty. Jesus came to reconcile us to God. He asks us to reconcile with God through faith. Reconciliation with God also means that we will be able to reconcile with each other. Our salvation brings a hope that does not disappoint. We can have hope that our relationships can see the same freedom and wholeness that we now enjoy because of the sacrifice of Jesus.

Proverbs 16:3 says, "Commit your actions to the Lord, and your plans will succeed." In prayer, express your desire to restore the relationship and commit your plans to God. Allow the Holy Spirit to guide you in what steps to take, whether it means writing a letter, making a phone call, stopping by the person's house, or whatever you feel is necessary. Maybe it is only continuing to pray for them until the time is right for face-to-face interaction. He will guide you.

Hold on to joy.

> "Don't copy the behaviors and customs of this world, but let God transform you into a new person by changing the way you think. Then you will learn to know God's will for you, which is good and pleasing and perfect." (Rom. 12:2)

The restoration process is not easy. It can take a very long time. In fact, in my own life, there is one relationship that comes to mind that has been broken for years. I have taken steps to reconcile but to no avail. However, I maintain the hope that one day I will be able to stand in front of this person and work toward the restoration and healing of this relationship.

We can rejoice in this difficulty because we are learning something in the process. We are learning something about ourselves, how to avoid pitfalls in other relationships, and potentially, how to humble ourselves to make peace.

Commit to peace.

> "Let the peace of Christ rule in your hearts, since as members of one body you were called to peace. And be thankful." (Col. 3:15)

"Work at living in peace with everyone, and work at living a
holy life." (Heb. 12:14a)

There is a difference between keeping the peace and making peace. Keeping
peace means that we will avoid, delay, acquiesce, and sometimes place ourselves
in a difficult spot all to "not make waves."

Making peace requires the hard work of swallowing our pride, no matter
how right we are, to come to a solution that benefits all involved. Most of the
time this does not come naturally. This is why I believe it is designated as a fruit
of the Spirit (Gal. 5:22). The desire for peace and the steps toward peace only
come through time spent with God, relying on His Spirit to guide us to the path
of peace.

Commit to love.

"Hatred stirs up conflict, but love covers over all wrongs."
(Prov. 10:12)

Allowing hatred or harboring a grudge is like cancer. Not only does it kill
the cells it infects, but it causes damage to the surrounding cells. In other words,
hatred, bitterness, and resentment will just drive you further into despair, and it
will infect all of your other relationships in a negative way.

Hope can reframe the conflict. It can bring you to the point of knowing
and understanding that conflict takes two opposing forces. Hate says, "you
don't need them anyway." But hope says, *"no conflict is too difficult for love
to overcome."* Hate says, "they hurt you way too bad ever to forgive them."
But hope says, *"no wrong is so wrong that love cannot cover it."* Believe in the
power of hope and love.

Commit to forgive.

"Be kind to one another, tenderhearted, forgiving one another,
as God in Christ forgave you." (Eph. 4:32)

No matter what someone has done or said to you, or what you have done
or said to someone else, forgiveness releases you from the continued hurt that
can affect you and others around you. If there is hope for us because God forgave
us through Jesus, then there can be hope for our relationships. We can choose to
forgive as Jesus forgave us. This is the most hope-filled statement we can hold
on to in our relationships.

If God can forgive us and we have much in our lives and hearts to be
forgiven for, in turn, we can share that forgiveness of wrongs done against us.

We should feel compelled to seek forgiveness and reconciliation when we have done someone wrong.

There is hope!

When going through a hurtful situation in a relationship, it can feel as if it will never be made right again.

Trust can be broken.

Words can leave emotional scars.

Thoughts can take you captive to the hurt.

But insert hope into the equation! What happens then?

Love for someone can cover over a multitude of wrongs.

Forgiveness can heal wounds left by words.

Trust can be rebuilt.

Thoughts can be forced into submission.

Restoration is possible.

We all have a responsibility in our relationships, even if we are not the one causing the relational damage. It is up to us to show love, model healthy conflict resolution, and do our part to make things right. No, you will not be able to control the response of the other person. But you can control your response, whether you are the hurt-er or the hurt-ee.

Sometimes you have to allow the other person to separate themselves for a time. They may need to go through a process before they are ready to re-enter the relationship. In that time period, pray for them. Ask God to bless them, be with them, and help them in their relationships.

I'm not someone who says that positive thinking will change anything except *your* attitude. However, there is a quote by author Robert H. Schuller that has helped me: "Let your hopes, not your hurts, shape your future."[11]

Hold out hope in your relationships. It is a powerful motivator. The next chapter expands on this.

16.

The Art of Humility

The ability to speak truth into someone's life only comes by permission and is most effective only through a relationship built on trust. But it absolutely requires a healthy dose of humility to both give and receive it.

I learned these truths through many friendships, but one of the most memorable times someone has spoken into my life came through my best friend from college, Brian Coscia. The University of Valley Forge (formerly Valley Forge Christian College) is a small university in rural Pennsylvania just outside of Philadelphia in a town called Phoenixville. The school only had about five hundred students in total when I arrived in 1992. Some of the best Philly cheese steak sandwiches were just across the street from the University at Bob's Haven Pizza & Deli. You could experience the best milkshakes on the planet at T.D. Alfredo's Pizzeria downtown in Phoenixville

The university was moved in 1976 to the former Valley Forge General Hospital on the property of a former military hospital base. The dorms were old buildings where some of the rooms may have been former offices, but most were former beds for patients. I am certain my first room at the school was a closet of some kind. It was at the end of the hallway just next to the door that led to the exit at the end of the building.

The men's dorms had community showers on each floor where six to eight showerheads lined the inside of a white-and-green-tile room. This is where I learned to take quick and efficient showers at the times when there were not a lot of guys going in and out.

Brian's room was at the other end of the hall and was a much larger room he had all by himself. We had no laundry room at the dorm, so weekly trips to the local laundry mat became customary. We would take our laundry to wash it, grab a pizza at the shop next door, and either do homework, talk, or just hang out.

If you are from the east coast, you will remember a convenience store named Wawa. Late at night, Brian and I would order a large pizza, and when we went to pick it up, we would make a Wawa run to get a drink and a pint of Ben & Jerry's ice cream.

I *cannot* imagine having half of a large 18-inch pizza and an entire pint of Ben & Jerry's now! I still cannot believe I shoved 2,000 calories in my gullet that late at night and still maintained a thin frame.

Brian and I became best friends. Our birthdays are in July only five days apart. There were not many things we did apart from each other. We talked and prayed together and confided in each other on many issues. We had a blast doing things we probably shouldn't have done. We played gin rummy, talked about girl issues, and studied together. We had some other friends we included in our circle as well, and we had a lot of fun with them too.

There was one boundary that I learned I should not cross with Brian, which I found out the hard way. I found out about this boundary when he and I stopped talking and hanging out to the point where we almost became estranged from each other. It probably lasted until about six months after our graduation.

This boundary had to do with a young woman. The perception on his part was that I was crossing the line between friendship and potentially "going for" the girl he was interested in. The fact was, I was friendly (and some would say flirtatious) to the point that I would lead some people to believe I was pursuing them. In one particular case, I was not respecting the relational line drawn in the sand with the girl he was interested in. It may have cost him this relationship. He had every right to be upset. Just because I could chalk it up to "this is how I am, and my intent was only to be friendly" didn't excuse the behavior.

I was so distraught over the fact that we had parted ways, so about six months after graduation I mustered up enough courage to call and ask for forgiveness for whatever it was that caused the rift between us. In that one conversation, we were able to reconcile our relationship.

SPEAKING AND RECEIVING TRUTH IN RELATIONSHIP

Since graduating in 1995, we have lived in separate parts of the country for most of our adult lives. But we do connect often. Brian invited me to be a part of his wedding in Ohio, and we also saw each other at a college reunion where we shared a motel room, even reliving the pizza and the Ben & Jerry's experience (big mistake). Every time we talk or get reconnected, it is like no time has passed. I trust him implicitly. He is one of three men that knows *everything* I have experienced since college and knows me maybe even better than I know myself. And when we talk, we don't really have to catch up as most friends do. We simply start sharing the good things we are experiencing and the areas where we need prayer. We know the trust is a solid brick wall, and it is easy to share without fear of criticism or rejection. We can each speak truth into the other's life and understand we have the other's best interest at heart.

I can't even begin to tell you how much my friendship with Brian has meant to me and the lessons I have learned because of it. One primary lesson is the fact that people in healthy relationships need to be able to speak and receive the truth about the hurts they have experienced, whether done on purpose or not.

My actions do affect others, sometimes positively, but other times negatively. Someone does not *have to* tolerate my behavior just because it is "who I am." Of course, they accept and love me for who I am, but my negative behavior does not need to be tolerated. Of course, I do not *need* to change to gain their acceptance. However, Jesus tells us that we need to *"love others as we love ourselves,"* which means I should ask myself how I would want to be treated before I plow forward and hurt my loved ones. Would I want them to respect my relational boundaries? *Absolutely!*

Changing my behavior does not mean I am changing who I am at the core. It means I am honoring someone else above myself for the sake of the relationship. Therefore, respecting relational boundaries, especially of a close friend, means accepting the fact that I can negatively affect the lives of others and lose a friend if I remain indignant that others *must* tolerate my behaviors that have negative consequences in the relationship. I'm so glad Brian was able to tell me truthfully what I had done so I could apologize and correct my behavior going forward. Which brings me to the second lesson I learned because of Brian.

SPEAKING TRUTH REQUIRES EMOTIONAL CONSENT

I'll never forget the night when I opened up and shared a deep secret with Brian over the phone. It was one of the hardest nights of my life. However, he was there with no judgment, just listening, encouraging, and not trying to fix it or me. He listened with a heavy concern for my well-being. That was a humbling night, to say the least.

We had another conversation over the phone (I cannot remember when) the details of which have been a constant reminder to me of the importance and command found in James 4:10—"to humble myself before God and in due time He will lift me up."

It was one of our semi-annual to quarterly check-ins. We were sharing our normal ups and downs, except this time Brian had to share something specifically with me regarding a dream he had. After my joking with him that the Bible said "old men will dream dreams," he began to share with the disclaimer that even though God speaks to us through dreams, this was not a criticism, but it was meant as an avenue for growth in my life.

Picture it.

Brian and I were backstage, where just around the curtain sat a large crowd of people. On the stage were angels with awards. They were handing them out to several recipients, two of which were Brian and me.

Brian was called onto the stage where the angel presented him with his award. The crowd cheered, and he graciously accepted the award and the applause.

The next name called was mine. Except that the angel who was presenting my award was only two to three feet tall. I walked out onto the stage to receive the award and had to kneel down next to the angel to accept it.

At this point, the dream ended. I asked Brian what he thought it might mean. He said, "I believe it means that God truly desires to give you what it is you are asking for, but for you to receive it, you need to humble yourself. If you humble yourself, God will bless you with what you are asking for." (He was referring to the need I expressed in the humbling conversation we had previously.)

At this point, I wish I could say I was falling over thankful for the words of rebuke and encouragement from my best friend. I didn't respond at the moment, but only thanked him for sharing his dream. Later, when I started thinking about it, I became upset.

"I am humbling myself!" "How could he say such things?" It took me several days and weeks to process and accept what I heard from Brian. As I began to soften my heart to the dream, a proverb rose to the surface, "Wounds from a sincere friend are better than many kisses from an enemy," (Prov. 27:6).

Here is the thing. Brian and I live several thousand miles apart. Why would he have any reason at all to share this dream with me other than to help me grow? As I continued to process this dream and what it might mean, I realized my pride was keeping me from seeing the significance.

I really needed to hear this message. I had been in a funk for a while, wondering why I was in the current ministry position that did not require me to use my passion to teach and speak. When I moved back to California, the opportunities were not coming very quickly, if at all. It took about three years (with a couple of opportunities to speak sprinkled in) before I started to have more invitations and opportunities to use this passion.

What I learned from this experience is that the ability to speak into someone's life *only* comes by permission. I had given Brian permission a long time earlier to speak into my life, and he had given it to me to speak into his life. If Brian and I had not developed a history of trust—implicit trust—with each other, the wound he inflicted by sharing this dream could have ripped a hole in our friendship. Something lacking in most leadership/mentoring relationship training is the idea of "emotional consent." This is vital to relational growth and to become a better leader.

Even though what he shared hurt, it was incredibly effective. I have remembered that conversation on more than one occasion. I am reminded of it every time I go onto a platform or a stage to speak or teach. It helps me remember that I am only the medium God has chosen for that moment to speak life into the people who are listening.

When Brian and I talk on the phone after six months or even a year, it is like we simply pick up the conversation where we left off. We do not have any issue sharing the hard points of our lives, or even any fear of how the other will respond. There are no inhibitions in our discussion. Gratitude for our friendship over the years and our love for God are crucial elements of our relationship. Along with one other significant factor—*humility*.

SPEAKING AND RECEIVING TRUTH REQUIRES HUMILITY

You see, Brian had asked permission to share that dream with me. He received my emotional consent. But it was in humility that he shared it. He didn't automatically expect that I should listen to him. I had given Brian the permission to speak into my life, so also in humility, I needed to listen, process, and allow God to work in my heart to receive the words that were spoken.

When developing friendships with others, it is incredibly important to remember that just because you are friends does not mean you have permission to rebuke or speak into someone's situation. It is healthy to ask permission ahead of time. This shows humility and respect for the other person.

I incorporate this concept into coaching sessions with others. Even though we have entered into an agreement, I never assume they want to hear what I have to say, especially if it is a rebuke or correction. I recognize that I may have the ability and power to do something, but I hold back for their sake. Asking permission to speak into someone's life after developing the relationship raises the level of effectiveness.

Humility is also about recognizing our place in this world. Andrew Murray wrote a book entitled *Humility*. In this book, he sums up pretty well the lesson on humility and how we should view it.

"Men sometimes speak as if humility and meekness would rob us of what is noble and bold and manlike. O that all would believe that this is the nobility of the kingdom of heaven, that this is the royal spirit that the King of heaven displayed, that this is Godlike, to humble oneself, to become the servant of all."[12]

Loving God helps us to know there is something so much bigger than us. It reminds us that without our Creator, life would not exist. Loving others helps us to understand we are not the *only* one God created. We are each unique and special to Him. If this is the case, we can love others, think of ourselves in sober judgment, and then truly focus on serving people, especially those in our own community. How are we exhibiting humility in our own relationships?

My actions do affect others...even those closest to me...especially those closest to me. There has to be emotional consent to share concerns or speak into another's life which comes only by building a solid relationship of trust. And humility is key to sharing and receiving the truth. These are the relational lessons I learned from Brian.

17

The Art of Influence

I was the ripe old age of twenty-two when I answered the call to go to Paterson, New Jersey. There was a medium-sized church on North 9th Street called "The Pentecostal Lighthouse." The church was a non-denominational community that had been solid for over eighteen years and had grown steadily during that time.

I met with the entire board of the church—eight men and women who all had a relationship with their senior pastor that was built on trust and one of the strongest displays of loyalty and respect for the man who had led them that I have ever seen since being in leadership.

I had spoken to many of them personally, and they each said the same thing about Victor Coetzee (kout'-see). He was a man that exemplified what it meant to be a leader.

The ages of the board of directors ranged from about thirty-five all the way to seventy. They each had a story to tell of how Victor Coetzee had impacted and influenced their lives. He had been there for them through crises, walked with them through tough ministry decisions, and took responsibility for when things went wrong.

Pastor Coetzee had led them for over seventeen years. The church was only about fifty people when he took over the reins of ministry there. In those seventeen years, he led them to over four hundred people. This growth for some may not be the most impressive. We have churches now that go from a few hundred to thousands in six months to a year.

However, most of the over four hundred people who attended the Lighthouse were a solid core of individuals that had been trained and given a strong foundation of teaching to endure life's trials to come out stronger. The church had persevered and weathered many storms. Pastor Coetzee had led them to truly become a lighthouse for God on the solid Rock, much like its actual position on the hill in the north side of Paterson.

Victor Coetzee had been born in Zimbabwe, formerly Rhodesia (as he would always say). He met his wife, Suzanne, and they became missionaries to Puerto Rico. They served there faithfully until answering the call to come to the inner city of New Jersey and take over a small church in Paterson.

By now, you probably have a picture in your mind of what he looks like. It may blow your mind to know that he was a white man from Africa, who had become a missionary to Puerto Rico (fluent in Spanish) and moved to the inner city to lead a small group of blossoming leaders. In his time there, he led one of the most diverse groups of people (in status, background, and ethnicity) that I have experienced to date.

It could not have been more strategic for him to be in this position. Paterson was one of the tougher cities in New Jersey where not many people chose to live. As a matter of fact, I always said growing up that I would never live in New Jersey. Yet there I was living twenty minutes west of Manhattan as a white kid from Maryland with *a lot* to learn. I learned more in the first year of ministry with Pastor Coetzee than I had in all my years prior.

Before getting recruited as the new youth pastor of the Lighthouse, the board had a stack of resumes on their conference table made up of two eight-foot tables. After hiring me, they each told me in their own way that my resume had just "risen to the top," and under the leadership of Pastor Coetzee, believed I was the person that God wanted for this church.

Even now, I believe it was this church that I needed. The example and growth for me personally, emotionally, and spiritually, especially during this first year outside of college, has shaped me and helped me to become the person I am today. Pastor Coetzee taught me some significant lessons about the art of influencing others, which I would like to share with you.

TEACHING BY EXAMPLE

One Saturday in May, in a park just north of where the church was located, the families of the church converged into this green space with trees, grass, and playground equipment. I met Pastor Coetzee there early and found him unloading a van full of chairs and tables.

Some might wonder why a pastor of this size church was doing manual labor. For me, I didn't ask. I just reached in and started to take the load and stand beside him. He could have delegated that responsibility, but he didn't.

In a way, though, he actually did. He was teaching through his actions. He was exemplifying what he wanted all of us to do. He didn't see himself as a leader above the work, but as a servant to all who God had placed under his leadership.

In that one moment, he solidified something I had witnessed my mother doing over and over. He did not think of himself as higher than he should, but taking on the very nature of a servant, served others. He was following the example of the One he had dedicated his life and ministry to—Jesus. People need to see action, not just hear about it.

LEADING THROUGH COACHING

That first year of ministry under his leadership, I made my fair share of mistakes. Through each mistake, he guided me much as a coach would. He didn't fix the issues I had created. He encouraged me and guided me to work the problem and build a solution.

He was incredibly patient with me and with so many others he led. He knew every aspect of the church. He took me on visitations to the hospital, houses, and even places of business. I watched and heard how he spoke and cared for the people we went to see. He turned to me and asked me to pray, to read a Scripture, or just to lay a gentle hand on someone to show we cared. Later my wife called this the "Pastor-Hand move."

He helped me develop the confidence in relationship with others where it did not matter that we made mistakes; it mattered how we handled them when they were made.

Little did I realize in that first year, the only year I worked alongside Pastor Coetzee, that he was grooming me to take on a role that was going to come as a surprise to me, but not him. Pastor Coetzee had begun to struggle with a disease that eventually took him from us, Parkinson's Disease.

AN EXAMPLE OF FAMILY

Pastor Coetzee invited me into his home on more than one occasion. He and Suzanne had created a family space that would amaze most people. Not only did he have a heart for people, but he and his wife had a huge heart for kids—kids that had been abandoned by their parents because of physical or mental disorders. They were foster parents for children that had special needs.

I remember Marcus. He was just a toddler. His mother had been addicted to drugs, and he didn't have a father to speak of. They took in Marcus, this child that lived with Down's Syndrome and many physical complications that required much time and attention. They loved Marcus like one of their own. At any given time in their home, you saw kids running around, Marcus climbing into Pastor Coetzee's lap, and the love pouring from them. Anyone that was brought into their home instantly became their family. They were inviting, welcoming, and wanted you to see their space as a place of love, healing, and joy.

Did the Coetzee family struggle? Absolutely. However, their example of perseverance and character produced hope in the many lives that were blessed to be around them for any length of time.

BEHIND-THE-SCENES INFLUENCE

During this first year, I spent many hours with the leaders of the church, the parents of the youth I was leading, and the youth that had started to come to the church. On more than one occasion, I heard about or could see the influence Victor Coetzee had on the lives and families I spent time with. They each had a story of a moment, a time frame, or just consistently how he had been there for them in life, prayed for them through a difficult season, or called or encouraged them through his messages and teaching through the years.

When I was brought there, Pastor Coetzee had given me the liberty to start this youth ministry and try my hand at many different ideas. Some failed miserably and others succeeded by the skin of their teeth. He stood by me and supported me through all of them.

There was one event that I was working toward, a concert for the youth in the city. He could see how much of a toll it was taking and how it may not have been the best road to have traveled down. He allowed me to walk down this road and offered suggestions and cautions through the entire thing. Not once did he say, "Don't do this!"

At one point in the planning, I could see the necessity to pull the plug and take the loss. He didn't say, "I told you so." He simply encouraged me in the decision and taught me to lead in a way where I accepted responsibility, admitted errors, and moved on to the next thing. I was building the art of influence.

His behind-the-scenes influence in my life and ministry helped to teach me even when he didn't say any words. As you can see, I highly respected this man and how God has used him in my life, especially in the area of influencing others. He lived in a way where others could see who he was. He didn't need to say it—he lived it.

INFLUENCE REQUIRES HUMILITY

After about a year of ministry under Pastor Coetzee, he came to me and told me that he would be retiring after nineteen years of ministry in Paterson and over forty years of ministry as a missionary and pastor. I was more than dumbfounded, to say the least, although I understood why he was retiring, as he and his family were moving to a dryer climate while he battled with Parkinson's. Then he told me he had recommended to the board that I take the place as interim pastor in the transition between senior pastors.

WHAT!?!?

I was twenty-three years old. I was about to enter into the next four months in a level of leadership that takes some people years and years to obtain. I didn't ask for it. It was one of the final lessons in influence and leadership Pastor Coetzee was giving me on his way to retirement.

I went from the church members and leadership looking to me to guide their youth, to guiding them through the transition of leadership. I was petrified, to say the least. I had guys fifty years my senior calling me "Pastor Danny" and looking to me for leadership! However, because of Pastor Coetzee's influence in their lives and in my life, they trusted I would follow God first and lead with His wisdom, not my own.

Influence requires humility.

INFLUENCE AND AUTHORITY ARE DIFFERENT

When you don't know what to do, you can take two paths—try it on your own strength, or in humility look to God and to the counsel of others to walk you through it. The natural tendency is to use your own strength and plow through. It was this natural tendency that I had allowed to overtake me just before Pastor Coetzee was about to leave. I will never forget that night. It was a Sunday night right after a service at the Lighthouse.

For some background information, about a month after he had announced his retirement and the transition began, I was making decisions as if I was the senior pastor. This doesn't sound too bad; however, I was making decisions that should have been made with the board and leadership of the church. Even worse, I was acting as if I didn't need their approval, after all, I was the "interim senior pastor."

Not so fast, Sparky.

Instead of using the "influence" I was taught, I had shifted to using the "authority" of the name and position. That Sunday evening after service, Pastor Coetzee asked me to join him in the church office privately. We sat down across from each other in office chairs. He looked at me and said the following,

> *"What is this I hear about the decisions you have been making and overstepping your authority? Let me remind you that I am still the senior pastor here until I leave. Remember that these*

*men and women are here **with** you to lead this community. You would do well to build a relationship with them, trust them, and bring them **with** you. Authority means nothing without influence."*

I had been successfully rebuked, and rightly so. I had allowed my fear of leading through this transition to guide my actions. As we so often do at times, we feel the more we take control in a relationship, the more we will "feel" as if things are going well.

Relationships cannot be successfully controlled. But they can be influenced. In leadership, sometimes the best we can hope for is that through relationship someone decides willingly to look to us because we have proven to them we care for them and have their best interests in our thoughts and decisions; that we are consistent in our lives and have a relationship with God.

After that much-needed conversation with me, he sat down with the board at the next meeting (his last with us) and passed the baton over to me as the interim senior pastor. At that moment, I watched as he used his *influence* with the leadership team to delegate *authority* to someone who probably did not deserve it.

I realized something important at that moment. If I could consistently live in relationship with others, thinking of myself soberly and with good judgment, people could decide to allow me to lead them. This relationship with them would make it easier to say, "I will walk with you. I will fight alongside you. I will support you. I will live life with you."

If my relationship with God is not in the right place, which takes consistency and persistence on my part, then I could not maintain focus on my relationship with others, serve them in humility, and lead them with God-honoring confidence in His ability to lead me.

I learned more in that first year of ministry outside of college than I had in all my previous years of education about relationships. Specifically, I had learned that influence is earned and that authority means nothing without influence.

OUR INFLUENCE AS SALT AND LIGHT

"You are the salt of the earth. But what good is salt if it has lost its flavor? Can you make it salty again? It will be thrown out and trampled underfoot as worthless. You are the light of the world – like a city on a hilltop that cannot be hidden. No one lights a lamp and then puts it under a basket. Instead, a lamp is placed on a stand, where it gives light to everyone in the house. In the same way, let your good deeds shine out for all to see so that everyone will praise your heavenly Father." (Matt. 5:13)

In the Scripture above, Jesus uses two metaphors to describe the influence that Christians have—salt and light. Both of these natural elements have amazing qualities that influence their environments. We can learn a lot about how we can influence the people around us by understanding their properties. Let's start with salt.

Salt influences everything it touches. If you put salt on a wound, it burns but also heals. If you put salt on food, it brings out the flavor of the food. Salt has so many uses. Reader's Digest has an article entitled "60+ Ways to Use Salt" by Trish Barber.[13] I picked out a few that can teach us something about how we use our influence to live in relationship with those around us:

- *Hold artificial flowers in place.* Fill a vase or container with salt, add a little cold water, and arrange your artificial flowers. The salt will *solidify*, and the flowers will stay put.

- *Eases fireplace cleanup.* When you're ready to turn in for the night but the fire is still glowing in the hearth, douse the flames with salt. The fire will burn out more quickly, so you'll wind up with less soot than if you let it smolder. Cleanup is easier, too, because the salt helps the ashes and residue *gather* into easy sweepings.

- *Restores sponges.* Hand sponges and mop sponges usually get grungy beyond use long before they are really worn out. To *restore* sponges to a pristine state, soak them overnight in a solution of about ¼ cup salt per quart (liter) of water.

- *Freshens your garbage disposal.* Is an unpleasant odor wafting from your garbage disposal? *Freshen* it up with salt. Just dump in ½ cup salt, run the cold water, and start the disposal. The salt will dislodge stuck waste and neutralize odors.

- *Speeds up cooking time.* In a hurry? Add a pinch or two of salt to the water you are boiling food in. This makes the water boil at a *higher temperature* so the food you are cooking will require less time on the stovetop. Keep in mind: salt does not make the water boil faster.

- *Revitalizes skin and boosts circulation.* Remove dead skin particles and boost your circulation. Either while still in the tub, or just after stepping out of the tub, while your skin is still damp, give yourself a salt massage with dry salt. Ordinary salt works well; the larger sea salt crystals also do the job.

Jesus tells us as believers that we also will influence anyone we come into contact with, including those we are in a relationship with or not, whether they are believers or not. God wants our influence to be useful, like salt, to *solidify* our relationships with other believers. He wants us to *gather* others and help *put out* the fires of conflict between us; to *restore* relationships and our own lives so we can be used by God. We can *freshen* up our lives and the lives of those around us and become more *effective* to *enhance* the relationships around us. God will *remove the dead areas* of our lives and *boost our spiritual circulation* so the body of Christ can operate without hindrance. Just as salt is useful, we can be, too.

Now, let's look at the properties and influence that light has on the environment. You'll see that light influences everything it reaches.

- Light *illuminates* the darkness. In fact, darkness cannot exist in the presence of light. Light helps us to *see* and *exposes* what is hiding in the darkness.

- Plants need light to *grow*. Through photosynthesis, plants need light to synthesize foods (energy) from carbon dioxide and water by turning them into carbohydrates.

- Humans need light to *avoid health issues* caused by Vitamin D deficiency, like depression, negative feelings, and impaired wound healing. Vitamin D is synthesized when sunlight touches the skin.

- We see objects and color but only because light allows us to receive these images through our eyes. In the darkness, there is the absence of color. In the light, we *see color* all around us.

- Light provides warmth, which is *energy* to many things. If it were not for the light of the sun, the delicate balance of life here on earth would be out of balance and not be able to exist.

- Lights are used as *signals* in many different areas of life—red lights, green lights, yellow lights, white lights, blue lights.

Just like light, we are to be shining the light of Christ into the lives of those around us. We can *illuminate* the darkness around us and bring *life* into our relationships because of our connection to the Light. We can bring *health* into our relationships because of the access to the Light, as well as bring *color* and *vibrancy* into the lives of others. We can give *energy* to others and raise the *signals* of right or wrong living to keep us traveling on the right path in life.

As the salt and light of the earth, Christians can influence those in our families, our friends, our co-workers, those who see us and watch us even from a distance, anyone we come into contact with, our church, and the world. Imagine if all of us as believers understood our own effectiveness in the influence we can have on the lives of others. We will influence everyone we touch and everyone we reach, whether positively or negatively. It is because of our relationship with God that we can influence others positively.

When we walk into a situation or room, do others immediately feel more stable, loved, cared for, and valued? Are the people around you better off because you are there? Be a light. Shine wherever you are. People are attracted to light.

Just like Pastor Coetzee, we can learn that our influence carries more weight than our authority, that influence takes time, and just like salt and light, it continues to work behind the scenes, improving everything it touches and reaches.

18.

The Art of Community

"Networking is rubbish; have friends instead."
~ Steve Winwood, Music Artist

There is a lot of wisdom in this quote by musician Steve Winwood. The difference between networking and a community of friends is huge in terms of relationship. One is done based on needing something from someone, the other is mutual and inclusive. Let's start with how networking is defined.

Networking is "the exchange of information or services among individuals, groups or institutions; specifically: the cultivation of productive relationships for employment or business," or it can be "the establishment or use of a computer network."

A computer network is made up of several to many computers used for a specific purpose. They are all connected to a central location for that information to pass through to get to another connected location. Computer networks can be connected to each other through the use of the internet. The internet is essentially the highway where information or services are transmitted. In this picture, networking is entirely mechanical and technological.

However, a community is a sort of relational networking among human beings. It is much more organic than networking. How? We decide who we wish to be connected to or not. We can stop the flow of information or services with any individual we want to. We can also decide to be connected to whomever we wish and begin the flow of information or services with any person. The power of community is way underestimated, in my opinion.

Communities have to be built, which requires time, intentionality, and trusting God with the opportunities. Why build community with others? Because we could be one relationship away from changing the course of our destiny. You never know when someone you meet has the key or connection or opportunity you've been waiting for that will propel you forward in life. Let me give you an example.

Ever since I was a teenager, I have been making connections; that is, building a community of people in every area I have lived. That community supports me and everyone around me. I never rely on just one or a few individuals. Some connections are stronger than others, but at any time, the lesser connections can be strengthened with time and relationship.

Even though I have been building a community of people around me for over thirty years, it wasn't until the last five years when I realized the extreme importance and imperativeness to always build on that community. What do I mean by this?

Wherever I have lived, Baltimore, near Philadelphia, inner-city New Jersey, Los Angeles, Central Coast California, or Northern California, my desire to get to know people on a personal level has always been present. By taking someone to coffee or lunch or just sitting down for a few minutes, you can learn a lot about someone when you ask the right questions. It begins a relationship with people. Plus, it means more to get to know someone than it does just to do a transaction and move on.

This is not difficult to learn, but for some, I realize it is difficult to do. It requires the art of listening and patience that has taken me quite a long time to master, and I still have a long way to go. Impatience is one of the viruses that can sicken any relationship.

Asking someone to tell you a little about themselves leaves too much room for the person you are talking to. This leeway allows the person to give you only the information they want you to hear. In most conversations they will paint a positive picture of their life, leaving out the areas where they may accidentally leak information that shows their insecurities and weaknesses, or even dreams and aspirations.

When I first meet someone, I usually ask specific questions as long as I have some time to sit down and listen. Sometimes I even have a pad and pen to take notes, which I ask them if it is okay to use. Taking notes increases my capacity to remember the information they are about to provide. Here are the typical questions I ask:

Where were you born and how did you get to where you are?

Where have you lived?

Why did you choose your current profession or place to live?

When someone begins to share their story, they may glide over information such as what elementary school they went to, or why they moved from Ohio to California when they were eight years old. It is at this point I may stop them and ask them to share a bit more about why they moved from one state or city to the next.

Here are a few more questions that assist in them sharing their journey or story:

What does your dad or mom do that caused the move?

Are your parents still living? If so, where are they and do you get an opportunity to see them often?

Why did you select the college/university you attended?

What was it about your spouse that drew you to them?

How did you meet your girlfriend/boyfriend/spouse?

Do you have any children?

How old are they and what are their names?

What is the best thing going on in your life right now?

What is something you are really looking forward to in your future?

Where was your favorite place you have visited in your travels?

When someone begins to share their story, inevitably they start to remember pieces of information they may feel are irrelevant to the conversation. Questions probe those pieces of information, and the answers can provide deeper insight into who a person is.

Each of us has a history unique to ourselves. *No one,* absolutely *no one,* has experienced the exact same combination of events, experiences, emotions, or evolution of thought. We try to place ourselves into categories, labels, and/or people groups, but the truth is, we are all different. We only share certain aspects of our history that connect us to a category.

You see, we are more than just what job we have. We are more than just where we live, the color of our skin, or the family we were born into. If we sit down with each other and build community and connections with others who we classify as "different" than us, we may be surprised how much we learn about them, and even ourselves.

The importance of building community cannot be overstated. Sure, there is some aspect of need. We should network to get what we need or want. But if we stop there, we are only thinking about us. Our community of relationships is powerful. In one instant, you may meet someone who has a need. A connection is revisited in your relationships, and you know that if you can connect this person to someone who can help them, then their need will be filled, thereby creating a connection that only deepens your network.

BUILDING COMMUNITY IN N. CALIFORNIA

In my adult life, I have moved seven times to a different city (a couple of moves I made were back to an area I had lived years before). Each time I have moved, whether by myself or with my family, I have had to build a new network of connections in that area. Keep in mind, I have kept my networks and connections from the areas I have moved from. I call it "expanding my community."

Expanding our community stretches our skills with people, increases our interactions and forces us to learn how to adapt to new situations. We can learn so much through this process, although it can be difficult. Plus, opportunity comes through relationship.

The most recent move to Northern California was no different. If anything, this was the most difficult transition. When we moved to Roseville, my wife and I knew no one. We had no business connections, personal connections, or friends we could call in an instant to help us move a piece of furniture, find out what the best restaurants are, and so forth.

We were starting from scratch, so I just reached out and set up my first appointment with a church where I was hoping to work to see if there was a position available. After church one Sunday, my wife and I met with a woman who filtered out people for the jobs at this large church in Northern California. Even though there were positions available, it was clear I was not who she was looking for.

This catapulted me into what became a season of planting seeds of relationship. It became clear that all throughout my life this was something I was practicing. It wasn't until this last move where mastering this skill—this art of community—became a possibility. I still do not believe I have mastered it, as I am always a student of relationship. However, it has become much easier to do. What I needed to do was build community with those I was trying to reach.

I began asking people to go to coffee. I would like to say this was easy at first. I had started a business/ministry called *The Sophos Group,* offering consulting, coaching, and support. My entire goal was to befriend pastors and leaders in business and become a friend to them—someone they could talk to, get to know, and be there as support personally and, if needed, professionally.

I made visits and phone calls to pastors. I walked into businesses and tried to get an appointment with a manager or owner. I did not take rejection too well. Actually, it really sucked, until I read an article about a man that decided for several months to ask questions of people where he knew he would receive a negative response. His goal was to learn how to handle rejection.

It is ironic. After I realized that rejection could be a closed door and that you just need to keep knocking on *other* doors to see which one would open (instead of knocking on the same door waiting for it to open...eventually), that is when my coffee/lunch times started to gain traction.

I took a couple of pastors for lunch or a coffee. Some pastors were very skeptical of me, to the point of inferring I was only trying to sell them something. Others would hear my heart and what I was trying to accomplish and offer advice on how to move forward. At each meeting I attended with a pastor or business person, they dropped names of people they felt like I should connect with and provided their contact info.

I called every single one. This was laying the foundation of what I could build on.

For the most part, people I called agreed to a meeting with me due to the name of the person who provided their info. I found myself having coffee or lunch several times per week, getting new names and meeting new people. Not every person I met has turned into a relationship. Not every seed you plant in a relationship will be sown in fertile soil. Some heart soil is already at capacity for relationships at that moment.

Through this process, I reconnected with a mentor of mine; I've mentioned him in another chapter, Steve Preston. His counsel and advice helped me immensely. Plus, rekindling a friendship just enriched our connection.

Very close to our arrival in Northern California, I reached out to the leader of the district of the denomination where I am ordained. His assistant helped me get on his calendar for lunch. He was not available for a couple months, so I set up a meeting with the district's secretary/treasurer. We sat in his office for over an hour getting to know each other. I started off with him like I did with everyone else: "Where were you born?" and "How did you get to where you are right now?"

After meeting with him, I met with the superintendent for lunch, which included the secretary/treasurer, at a Mexican restaurant close to their offices. Because of what I was trying to accomplish in ministry, they recommended I meet with Dr. Sam Huddleston, the Assistant Superintendent of the Northern California District of the denomination.

My reason for meeting him up front was to let him know about the ministry I was starting in Northern California. From that initial meeting, he invited me to join him on a trip to Burney, California with a pastor from Cuba who oversees the Assemblies of God there. This trip was to attend a men's conference where I found out that I would be speaking for thirty minutes the next day to a group of about one hundred men. Talk about always being prepared!

This relationship that began with Dr. Sam has continued and grown stronger each time we meet. He invited me to be part of the District Men's Ministries Board, which assists in decisions for the annual men's conference where about 1,500 to 2,000 men attend each March. This opened up and continues to open up more opportunities to expand my community with other pastors and leaders in ministry.

A month before that conference invitation, I was walking in my neighborhood to get fresh air and to think. I really wanted to get connected into the business community and marketplace in the greater Roseville area but didn't know how I was going to break through the barrier of not knowing anyone at all. During the walk, it hit me, "Why not email the mayor of Roseville?" "Who was the mayor?" "I wonder if she would respond to my email?"

My next thought was, "It never hurts to ask!"

That's what I did that night. I sat down, wrote an email introducing myself and my wife, letting her know that we were new to Roseville, and we wanted to build community in the marketplace. I hovered over the send button for about five minutes while re-reading the email for content and spelling. Then I did what seems natural but can be very difficult when taking a chance; I hit send.

The next day, while checking my emails, I saw a response from the mayor of Roseville. She had taken the time to write me back. It wasn't a form email. It was thought out and included an invitation to coffee for my wife and me at a local coffee house named Bloom Coffee & Tea.

We met her on July 31, 2014. She spent an hour with us and didn't rush off even though she had an appointment. Mayor Susan Rohan understood the importance of relationship. When I mentioned my desire to get involved in the marketplace and get connected, she recommended two things. One, she suggested getting involved in the Roseville Chamber of Commerce (of which I was already on that path).

Second, she recommended I attend a Rotary Club lunch where around one hundred business leaders from the greater Roseville area gather for a lunch event every Thursday from 12 p.m. to 1:30 p.m. To my surprise, she connected me through text message to one of the former mayors of Roseville, Jim Gray.

On to the next connection to expand my community!

My father-in-law was involved in Rotary in the central coast of California for over twenty-five years. One of the pieces of advice he had given to me was to join the Rotary Club, where relationships would take on an entirely new level and provide insight into the community.

I attended several lunches and spent time getting to know Jim Gray, as well as inviting many others to coffee or lunch to get to know them. Within four months, I was inducted into the Rotary Club of Roseville, which immediately expanded my community, not only here in Roseville, but to the hundreds of people I have met since being invited to join.

In two years of being a part of Rotary, I have served on many committees, volunteered at many events and community service projects, and was asked to be the Public Image Chairperson for the local club.

I will never forget the advice of a man named Jim (a former ambassador for the Roseville Chamber of Commerce, who has since passed from this life). His advice was this, "Dan, the best advice I can give you is to *be present*. Be *in* the mix. No one can see who you are and what you do if you are not physically present at functions, meetings, or events." Whether you are an introvert or an extrovert, being "present" where people can see you exist and know your name is critical to opportunity through relationship.

Since coming here to Roseville in 2014, the number of connections we have made and the expansion of our community has been exponential.

So many believe that if they can set up a business, church, ministry, or event, people will just show up at the door wanting what you have to offer. It took almost two years of planting the seeds of relationship in this network to see any visible fruit. I can remember times where I was so frustrated with what seemed like stalled forward movement that I asked God if He even remembered He had created me.

I so desperately wanted to make a difference and be an influence in the lives of others. My impatience with the planting, watering, and nurturing process got to me at times. Whenever that happened, I would go into a pity-party mode. Then I would snap out of the funk I was in and begin to plant more seeds of relationship.

A farmer will continually plant seeds throughout the year in different areas of the land. This is because he wants to keep a harvest of his crop moving in various areas throughout the coming months. Just because he may plant a field of broccoli, doesn't mean that broccoli will sustain them for the rest of their lives.

In our relationships, we can be satisfied with an "us-four-and-no-more" mentality. This is where we don't expand our community beyond those who are immediately around us, those we get along with the best, and we enjoy the seemingly solid state of our group. That is until something changes in the group.

We should still stay connected and nurture those relationships. However, realizing we have more capacity for more relationships is critical to branching out with other people.

Trusting God for the Results

One thing I have learned over the years is that I could never have orchestrated or planned how the relationships I have developed would have looked or taken shape. There is a *huge* element in this process I haven't mentioned yet.

I fully believe that when we connect with others, God will use us and those in our community of relationships to benefit those around the greater community. This enhances the relationships in the community. Eventually, this will positively influence those who will become a part of that greater community because of our willingness to reach out way beyond what we think we are capable of.

We will never know how God can use us in that way unless we make the decision to reach out and plant the seeds of relationship with others. Praying about how we can do this will open up opportunities you may have never noticed before.

One of the main reasons I began this book was because of the advice of someone I recently connected with when our communities collided. It was over coffee one summer afternoon where Roger Flessing, a man with an incredible community of relationships, said the one thing that I needed to inspire me to write in a way I had never thought of.

We both wanted to get to know each other and our life/faith journeys. We went to coffee and BOOM! From that one conversation, I had the key that I needed to fulfill a lifelong desire to write and complete the work you are reading now. It was so simple! And I am trusting God with the results.

One more connection loop...a friend named Charlie Harrison, who joined the Rotary Club of Roseville just a couple months before me, played golf and met a gentleman named Scott Lewis. Charlie and I had taken time to get to know each other over coffee. While playing golf with Scott, he determined that Scott would be a great person for me to get connected with. He mentioned my name to Scott, and he was interested in connecting.

The ball was now in my court. I contacted Scott, and we met for coffee at a local spot. When he came in, he laid his phone down on the table and told me to check out the app he had opened. It was a pre-release app for Museum of the Bible—a non-profit started by the Green Family who own and operate the major national craft store Hobby Lobby.

He had my attention.

Scott invited me to come to Los Angeles for an awareness event for the museum to gain support for the project. I could not pass up the opportunity to get in front of people I would never have dreamed of being in front of.

When I walked in, I met a man, and we exchanged life journeys while mingling before the event. He happened to be the one who wrote, directed, and produced the movie *Barbershop*.

When the event was about to begin, a friend of his came in, and he introduced me to him. His name is Dave Drever, and get this—Dave lives just down the road from me in Northern California, a mere six-hour drive from where we met in Hollywood.

The reason why I mention this story, which at this point has no end to it, is because it is a current story playing itself out all because of being obedient to what I believe God was asking me to do; that is, to get connected and take every opportunity to build relationship and expand my community. All of this started because I connected with people. The story goes on, and I am so glad to be a part of it.

Don't underestimate the effectiveness and power of expanding your community of friends and connections. All it takes is some time, intentionality, asking some good questions, a listening ear, and allowing yourself to know others and be known by them. From this, you will be surprised at how the hand of God is working, even though it may take time.

Building a community is more than just making an infinite number of connections. It is being an influence for Christ in as many arenas as possible, which gives you more opportunity to be an extension of God's hand in this world. Plant seeds of relationship. Be patient. Nurture these new relationships and stay connected to the ones you have always had. Pray and trust God to work through them.

19.

The Art of Love

*"Love is the feeling you feel when you feel you are going
to have a feeling you haven't felt before."*
~ Author Unknown

A hhhhhhh, love!

What comes to your mind when you hear the word *love?*

Romance? Emotions? A honeymoon? Funny feelings in your tummy?
Kissing? Hugs?

Interestingly enough, I put this phrase into Google, "first thing you think
of when you hear love," and the first link to pop up was a Yahoo Answers link.
Here are some of the answers it gave, in no particular order:

Fairytale

Anger, pain, and sadness

...being hurt

It's an illusion

What IS it?

What was your first thought?

For the most part, we have allowed our society to dictate to us what love is.
The first thing we must realize is that love has no working definition. What?!?!
Try to define it, and someone else will come up with another definition entirely
different than yours. Also, some of us define love based on our own experiences, whether positive or negative. Some would define love as "hugging your
children," while another might say "what you feel on your wedding day." The
two are *very* different emotions/feelings. Some may even define love as a sexual
relationship or attraction. But is this love?

Here is my response to all of these. Love is not *any* of these things!

So, what is love? (And cue song... "baby don't hurt me, don't hurt me, no more...")

Great question! I'm glad you asked.

First, let me describe what love is *not*...it is not an emotion. It is not a feeling. It is not sex. It is not getting what you want all the time.

But love *is*...a behavior, an action, a decision, a commitment. Love is a choice; it is active, not passive—it's not just something you fall into. You cannot *fall* in love. Allow me to demonstrate. Let's say you are standing on the edge of a cliff and down below about twenty feet is a pool of water. You are contemplating jumping off into the cool water, but you hesitate. Finally, you decide it is worth the risk and you make the decision to jump in.

Now, imagine you are on that same cliff, looking at the same water. You trip and fall tumbling over the side into the cool water. What is your first reaction? Is it one of elation? Or are you unsure of what is happening and how it will end up? Will you be pleasantly surprised? Or will you wish you had not fallen in, and you claw your way out of the water?

Which do you have more control over? Yes! The first one!

At least if you make the decision to jump in, you have some idea of what you are getting yourself into. You make the commitment, and you jump, understanding there are some things you may not be aware of, like how cold the water is or how deep the water is, but nonetheless, you go for it.

That is how it is with love. We *choose* who to love, when to love, where to love, and how to love.

The best example of love I can point to is Jesus.

In the face of a certain, imminent, painful situation that one could ever be faced with, Jesus chose to become the sacrifice for our sins. He had the opportunity to walk away from an excruciating death. Why would someone choose that kind of pain and torture? Because he was driven by love for us. That's right! He realized that from out of that painful circumstance, a way would be paved for us to have a personal relationship with God. Jesus had a choice to make, and he chose love.

So, what is love like? Scripture defines it for us in 1 Corinthians 13:4–13. Paul provides some particular qualities that identify love.

> *Love is patient.* When you are faced with a situation where you just want someone to realize you are there for them even though they make it difficult. Patience is an act of love.

Love is *kind*. When you would rather respond in vengeance, but instead you decide to show kindness, this is an act of love.

Love *does not envy, does not boast, is not proud*. You make a choice to be content with what you have, to be thankful for others, and to look at yourself with sober judgment—love.

Love is *not rude*. When your first reaction is to be sarcastic and snarky, but you decide to lock up the lips, you have expressed love.

Love is *not self-seeking*. If you actually look out for the needs of others, not just your own, this is loving others.

Love is *not easily angered*. Ouch, that one hurt a little, didn't it? It takes a decision to love to suppress the anger that rises so quickly to an unwelcome event or comment.

Love *does not keep a record of wrongs*. When you are in a disagreement, this is the decision *not* to bring up all of the past hurts or offenses the other person has done against you. Love is a continual choice to forgive.

Love *does not delight in evil but rejoices with the truth*. Have you ever heard gossip that you know is not true? Love is when you choose to push away the lie and gossip to stand with the truth.

There are qualities of love that should *always* be present. If these qualities are *not* present in an action, a relationship, or a decision, then it is not love!

Love *always* protects.

Love *always* trusts.

Love *always* hopes.

Love *always* perseveres.

If you love someone, you choose to protect them; you choose to trust them; you choose to hope for the best; you choose to persevere through difficult challenges. If we put all of these into effect, we can always count on love. It will not fail us.

Now, how many of these are dependent on the recipient of your love? If you answered "none of them," you would be correct. As much as you decide to show these qualities, others must also decide if they want to show them to you. However, you do not need them to be reciprocated to love someone. This means we can choose to love a complete stranger and provide a need for them. We can choose to love someone that has been rude to us.

Love is a choice to be committed to someone else; to place ourselves in a vulnerable position with them. When we look at it this way and not as if we are "falling in love," we recognize that if we choose to love, we can also choose not to love.

Emotions come and go. They are unstable. I *wish* I could stay happy all the time, but inevitably something will happen where I become sad. Love does not have to be as unstable as our emotions. As a matter of fact, Jesus showed how stable love really is by loving us before we ever accepted him as the Son of God and the One that takes away our sins. He loved us while we were denying his existence. He loved us while we were living our lives for ourselves. Maybe this is how we are to love others. By Christ's example, we can love others like that too.

A Brief History

I want to dig a little deeper into the meaning of love by giving some historical background on what was going on in Corinth at the time the apostle Paul wrote 1 Corinthians 13. I think it will help clarify what Paul meant by love.

Julius Caesar re-founded the city of Corinth in 44 B.C. as a Roman colony. He saw an opportunity to link the two bodies of water on either side of the three-mile isthmus of Greece with a canal—the Corinth Canal.

When revived as a Roman colony, it was populated by freed slaves for the most part, who came from Syria, Judea, Egypt, Greece, and other parts of the Roman world. They brought their expertise with them, which made them valuable: technical, administrative, financial. Now they were free to exercise their talents for their own benefit. With their combined knowledge and expertise, Corinth became a shipping center, bringing with it economic growth, business investors from around the Mediterranean, and lots of money!

The population of Corinth in the apostle Paul's time was about 250,000 free persons and 400,000 slaves. The culture, although under Roman rule, held a very Greek influence, concerning philosophy and its value in wisdom.[14]

Corinth had at least twelve temples, two of which were the temple to Aphrodite, the Goddess of Love, whose worshipers practiced religious prostitution, and the temple to Asclepius, the God of Healing. They were very mixed regarding religion. Along with the religious temples, especially the one to Aphrodite, immorality was practiced and celebrated. At one particular time in its history, about one thousand prostitutes served at the temple. Corinth became so widely known for its immorality, the Greek verb "to Corinthianize" came to mean "to practice sexual immorality."[15]

Why go through this information on a chapter about love? Corinth marks a very similar resemblance to where the United States is now. Although we do not have a temple where one thousand prostitutes serve in sexual immorality, the idea that intimacy is reduced to a sexual experience, or to take what love is and reduce it to a feeling or a sexual encounter, produces a generation (or two, or three) that looks at love as something that fluctuates and depends on how someone *feels* toward another. If I "fall out of love" with someone, I can just find someone else to "fall in love" with.

So, Paul sends his letters to the Corinthians, a chapter of which is dedicated to love. We call it the "Love Chapter" of the Bible. It is called this because the theme of this chapter does, in fact, have to do with love. We must, however, understand why Paul decides to move his letter to Corinth in such a direction.

Apparently, some believers in the church at Corinth were seeking some sort of status through the gifts of the Holy Spirit. Many people were seeking the gifts to get noticed and to bring attention to themselves. All of these motives have to do with ourselves and not with others. They were not based in love—they were very self-seeking.

In answer to those people who may have been seeking the gifts of the Spirit with the wrong motives, Paul says in verse 31 of chapter 12, "Eagerly desire the greater gifts." In other words, it is okay to desire those gifts that seem to be more public. However, we are not to seek them for our own benefit or for any of the glory, but to edify or to build up others in the family of God, the body of Christ, the church—and to do so in love.

Then Paul says, "And now I will show you the most excellent way." Chapter 13 exists here because Paul desired to show the Corinthians, and now us as we look into it, the correct way to exercise all spiritual gifts. We are to exercise them in love toward others.

Notice how he does not refer to love as a gift of the Spirit but as a *fruit* of the Spirit. A fruit by definition is something that is produced. What is it produced from? It is produced from the life and work of the tree firmly rooted in good soil. Good fruit can only come from a tree that has good nutrients, water, and a constant source of the sun.

If our lives are rooted in Christ, in his love, and in his sacrifice, and we receive our sustenance from his word, his life, his truth, and his light, we will produce good fruit. Love will be evident in our lives for God, for ourselves, and especially for others. Through our lives and through what we do for the Lord, love should be the motivating factor for what we do for others.

If I have not love, all I do is for nothing (vv. 1–3)

Paul lists the different gifts of the Spirit as hyperbole to help us understand the extent to which love should be our motivating factor to help others.

- "If we could speak in all the languages of the world and even in the language the angels speak, if we do not do so in love, we are nothing but noise."

- If we "have the gift of prophecy and can fathom all mysteries and all knowledge, and if I have a faith that can move mountains, but have not love, I am nothing." He says this to communicate the amount and level of understanding one may possess. If you don't have love, you are nothing.

- You could give all your earthly possessions to the poor and even die by being burned at the stake (a punishment brought upon many Christians during that time of persecution), but if you don't do it in love, you have gained nothing.

The Greek use of the word "love" here in this chapter specifies a selfless concern for the wellbeing of other people that is not brought on by any attribute of beauty in the person being loved. It is the product of a will to obey God and to love others as we would love ourselves. It is a choice.

It is like Jesus' love for us as he died on the cross. He loved us by doing it. Jesus said, "So now I am giving you a new commandment: love each other. Just as I have loved you, you should love each other. Your love for one another will prove to the world that you are my disciples" (John 13:34–35). He chose to love us.

Love described (vv. 4–7)

So often, we see love described as a feeling, an emotion. We hear of song lyrics like, "All I need is love," "I second that emotion," "When a man loves a woman," "I just called to say I love you," "What's love got to do with it," and more. In the movies, love is taught to us as being something that when lost, we cease to need the person who was the recipient of our love. This whole description of love from the world is a distorted view of what God meant for us to understand.

If we were to do a study on servanthood, we would learn that love is not a feeling. As a matter of fact, Jesus said himself in John 15:12–13, "My command is this; Love each other as I have loved you. Greater love has no one than this that he lay down his life for his friends." Jesus wants us to imitate his love for us to other people. This is a selfless love that does not rely on the response of the other person to exist to have an effect.

True love is love that does not wait for someone to show their love to you before you show your love to them. Jesus died for us first, therefore showing how much he loves us through his actions. We are to love others this way.

Love will remain! (vv. 8–13)

"…prophecies…will cease, …tongues…will be stilled, …knowledge…will pass away." These three are partial in nature and are needed while we live on this earth. These are ways in which the Lord can communicate to his church.

In verse 10, the word "perfection" in the Greek carries with it the meaning of "end," "fulfillment," "completeness," and "maturity." It refers to the day when we are standing before the throne of God, when we see Jesus face-to-face. This is the only time when prophecy will no longer be needed, tongues will not be needed, and knowledge will not be required, because he who is all-knowing, yesterday, today, and forever will be right before us.

The only thing that will be left is love—love for God and love in relationship with others.

Take notice of how Paul says, "for we know in part and prophesy in part, but when perfection comes, the imperfect disappears." Perfection will only come when we are with the Perfect One in Heaven. When Jesus comes, "perfection comes," and then and only then will the imperfect disappear. When we are in the presence of Jesus in Heaven, our bodies will be new, and our sinful nature will be gone entirely.

What we see and experience in our daily lives is a distorted, dim view of what love is. Paul takes two analogies "with childish ways" and "the reflection in a mirror" to help us understand that while we are on this earth, we only know Jesus in part. However, when we see Jesus face-to-face in Heaven, we will know him fully, even as we are fully known by him.

Faith and hope are essential in our walk with the Lord and relationships with others. But love? Love is the greatest and will remain forever. Why? Because God is love (1 John 4:16). He chose to love us. We can choose to love Him and love others. Discovering the lost art of relationship absolutely requires the building block of love.

I Love You, But I Don't Agree with You. Now What?

Is it possible to love someone and not agree with them on deep beliefs? At face value, we would probably say "yes" immediately. However, when put into a position to live it out, we might have difficulty showing that love.

Take a minute and think about the relationships you have in your life. Think about how many people surround you who hold the same basic, fundamental beliefs as you. Think about a family member who has taken a path or who made a decision that you just cannot reconcile or agree with. Think about a friend who announced to those closest to them something that goes against your core beliefs. I will not offer any examples of what these items can be. I am sure you can fill in the blanks with many different ideas, paths, beliefs, life choices, and so forth.

Now…what was your response?

Did the announcement, discussion on beliefs, action, decision, or even argument cause you to make a choice about your relationship and how you would approach them going forward? Did this keep you from loving them? How did your attitude change due to any one of these issues? Did you find yourself talking, calling, or responding to the family member or friend less often because of the disagreement?

It is a difficult situation. It is so much easier to avoid someone you disagree with even though you love them than it is to confront the situation, disagreement, or belief, and come to a place where you agree to disagree.

The question is, do you really ever stop loving that person? Is it possible to love someone you disagree with on a fundamental level?

My answer is this—it really depends on you. It is *possible*. It comes down to how you define "love" and how you decide to live your life in relationship with others.

Love is probably one of the most misunderstood, miscommunicated words in history. When you see someone overcome adversity and forgive others who have wronged them, you begin to understand that love is more than just a feeling.

As stated earlier, love is choice, an action, a behavior, a daily decision to be committed to another human being no matter the obstacle in that relationship. There are no criteria that have to be met for you to love someone.

"What? I don't believe you! What about the difference between marriage and friendship? What about the difference between loving your child or loving your spouse?"

Let me explain.

At the beginning of any relationship, whether it is a friendship with a colleague, a neighbor, the beginning of a marital relationship, or raising a child, you have a choice to make. That choice is to dedicate your time, talents, and a part of your life to spend for the benefit of another.

The only difference in the relationships I just mentioned is how you manifest them. In a marital relationship, the level of intimacy shared will be completely different (or should be) from a friend that you spend time with on occasion and share some of your life with. The love you show your children will be stronger in its manifestation especially when it comes to protection.

Each day, whether we realize it or not, we decide to love. Does this mean we can choose not to love others? That would be correct. This may be a simple description of love, and some may even think that I am way off base. Even though this sounds simplified, its execution is much more difficult.

Bringing us back to the question at hand: Is it possible to love others even if we disagree with some fundamental belief they hold or with a decision they have made? If you define love by your feelings, then any situation that brings a bad feeling your way will make you second guess your relationship with anyone. If you define love by your level of commitment to someone, then when a difficult conversation needs to happen, and you cannot find any middle ground, agreeing to disagree may be your only option. However, this should not stop you from loving them.

The closest we can get from truly understanding this concept of love as a commitment and being able to love even in disagreement is a parent to a child. When you have a child, whether, by birth or adoption, you raise that child, care for that child, and want the best for that child. When your child disobeys you or makes a decision that puts them and maybe others in jeopardy, you don't stop loving them. You may be disappointed. It may even hurt you to see them make decisions that you believe are detrimental to them or their future, but you don't stop loving them. You may have to have a confrontation or a difficult conversation. This may even drive that child further from you emotionally, but it's worth the risk.

A consistent decision and behavior that shows you love someone even in disagreement will win out in the long run. You may never see eye-to-eye on whatever it was that tried to come between you, but loving someone as a decision or an action, regardless of their response, will release you of any responsibility for their own reactions. Granted this takes an extraordinary amount of discipline. We would rather have people around us who don't take as much work to love. You know what I am referring to. These are people who hold the same common core beliefs, have the same values, and may even look like us.

Having others around us who believe what we believe, think in similar ways, and in whom we have much in common is so much easier than developing a friendship or relationship with a friend or family member who believes that for you to love them, you need to agree with everything they believe in. Love is sometimes described as a "two-way street." Although I believe a relationship is so much more meaningful when the love you show others is reciprocated, it is not necessary when it comes to loving another human being by our actions.

> "Love is patient. Love is kind. It does not envy, it does not boast, it is not proud. It does not dishonor others, it is not self-seeking, it is not easily angered, it keeps no record of wrongs." (1 Cor. 13:4–5, NIV)

Put these principles to work in your love toward others. It is a daily, continual decision that in the end will benefit you inwardly. What you will find is that you will develop meaningful relationships with many people...and not just those that you are most comfortable being around.

Choose to love...

20

The Art of Structural Integrity

Structural integrity: The ability of something to hold together under its own weight and whatever load is placed on it or in it.[16]

Each building is designed to hold its own weight of construction and anything placed inside of it. I'm sitting in my home right now and trusting that those who built the house followed the design of the architect, put enough screws and nails in place, and built the house without "cutting corners." If the house is not built to withstand its own weight, then a strong wind or even the furniture I put inside can weaken its connections and cause it to crumble—with me inside of it.

Tom Wujec, the founder of The Wujec Group and frequent TED Conference speaker, designed a teamwork challenge called the "Marshmallow Challenge." Teams were given twenty sticks of spaghetti, one yard of tape, one yard of string, and one marshmallow. They had eighteen minutes to build the tallest free-standing structure that could hold the weight of the marshmallow on top. The marshmallow could not be eaten or divided up into different parts, but they could utilize all the other items to build the tallest structure that would hold the marshmallow.[17]

Sound easy? Think again. This challenge has been given to executives, CEOs, teachers, college students, and even kindergartners. Which group do you think scored the best?

The kindergartners!

Actually, the teams that scored the highest were architects and engineers, but among all the others, kindergartners scored the best. They understood that the structural integrity of the spaghetti/tape/string tower was best when the structural integrity of the team was sound. How can that be?

With kindergartners, no one was trying to gain power. No one was trying to be the one who got the credit. There was the task, the team, and the goal to be the highest tower to win the prize. They also were not afraid to try different things to get the tower higher by using prototypes.

There is something to this...

So often the leader of a group gets the "glory" or the "credit" for the completed goal or the ongoing success. Don't get me wrong. It takes creative, inspirational leadership to keep a team moving in the right direction, but that is only one part of the structure. The entire structure needs to be built in such a way that the team can withstand its own weight (all of the personalities on the team), a strong wind (pressures from outside influences, unforeseen setbacks to the goal, people leaving the team, new people coming on), and the furniture that we put inside (the systems and processes we put in place to set the scene when we work together).

The point is this—relationships are only as strong as the structure it is built upon.

When relationships are healthy, mutual respect is shown. When each person works according to his or her strengths and complements the weaknesses of others, harmony happens. That harmony creates the environment by which people can work toward a common goal and not worry about who rises to the top or who takes the lead. It is an environment where people understand the integrity of the team is necessary and needs to be protected.

Are there perfect relationships? Absolutely...*not!* However, some relationships can withstand the test of time, adversity, and emotion.

Why? Because of the "Principle of Structural Integrity"—that is, the ability to hold something together under its own weight and whatever load is placed in or on it. Instead of spaghetti, tape, and string though, we use trust, vulnerability, love, hope, support, respect, honesty, forgiveness, gratitude, good communication, connection, purpose, authenticity, and a host of others things as the relational building blocks for long-lasting relationships.

These lifetime relationships are the kind that the Great Architect, God Himself, intends for us to have. His purpose in creating us is to be in a relationship with us and us with each other. If you desire a strong, structurally-sound relationship with anyone, it has to be built using these characteristics so that it can hold together and withstand whatever load is placed upon it, whether externally or emotionally.

If we build our relationships and teams on ego, misunderstandings, miscommunication, pride, or position, they will not have the healthy foundation necessary to continue through the challenges that will inevitably ensue.

I mentioned the idea of using prototypes for the Marshmallow Challenge above. A prototype is an original or first model of something from which other forms are copied or developed; a first or early example that is used as a model for what comes later.[18]

The kindergartners created a prototype early on during the eighteen minutes they were given. This gave them something to build upon. They used the marshmallow at each stage of the process to see whether their structure could withstand the weight of the marshmallow and then used that prototype to build it even higher.

Almost all of the other teams built their structure and at the very end of the eighteen minutes decided to put the marshmallow on top only to find that their structure was not able to hold the marshmallow. A crisis followed, and people had to act fast to try to beat the clock.

When teams were introduced to the idea of a prototype and incentivized with a prize at the end, teams excelled in this process. They understood that collaboration was more important than who had the idea—they worked together and developed stronger structures.

This whole idea sounds silly until we look at our own relationships. What prototype or model do our relationship(s) with others follow after? Are we building on a healthy prototype, or are we going down the path of relationship and it collapses because someone placed a marshmallow on it—they introduced a challenge, difficulty, or a heavily-weighted issue?

Jesus gave us the perfect prototype for healthy relationships in the Scriptures. He offered us the example of building relationships based on humility and the fruits of the Spirit, which are by-products of being connected to God and being "one" in unity with Him. When we are *in unity* with God, His relational attributes will not only be evident, but should become the foundation of all our relationships—love, joy, peace, patience, kindness, goodness, faithfulness, gentleness, and self-control (Gal. 5:22–23).

Each one of these fruits is foundational to healthy relationships. All of them have to do with how we react to others, but only one of them defines for us what our response should be, not our reaction—self-control. It takes self-control to respond with love, joy, peace, patience, and so on.

What would it look like if our relationships at home, work, friendships, and so forth, were structurally sound? We only need to look at Jesus. We can be sure that a relationship based on the example of how Jesus lived would be able to withstand whatever weight is placed on it.

Think about a bridge, like the Golden Gate in San Francisco, California. Let's say that a relationship is also like a bridge. A bridge spans a gap between two people just like a relationship. The gap between two people, the things that separate them, could be distance, race, socio-economic status, religion, politics, and so on. To bridge that gap, it needs to have several things. Footings or supports, decking, and suspension cables. Think of each person on each side of the gap as a footing, which needs to be grounded in a foundation that is deep enough to support the weight of the bridge, the relationship. This requires both people to dig way down deep to uncover many things in their life they may prefer to keep hidden, such as sin, evil, or selfish desires. Then they need Jesus to replace what they are digging out with a stable, strong footing or support that can hold the bridge (relationship) when the waves of life come crashing in (1 Cor. 3:11).

Only when two people have done the hard work of shoring up their own foundation, digging deep into the bedrock to provide stability for the relationship, can they then begin to span the gap with the decking, using for its support suspension cables that will hold the relationship in place. These suspension cables are the fruits of the Spirit mentioned before, and also things like trust, vulnerability, humility, support, respect, honesty, and forgiveness.

Any relationship built with God as the foundation is structurally sound. Its structural integrity will stand the test of time, and the relationship will endure against the elements of life that come crashing against the supports, including the winds of change that blow against it (Luke 6:46–49).

How structurally sound are the relationships in your own life? Are they built on trust, teamwork, collaboration, and mutual respect? Do they reflect the fruits of the Spirit? Spend some time today reflecting on a few of your key relationships to see if any building blocks need your attention. Any time spent strengthening your relationships is time well spent.

21.

The Art of Trust

Most of us would like to believe we are experts at reading people. Some people have this gift, however, more often than not, it is a challenge to truly know who a person really is until after you spend a lot of time with them.

I used to believe that all people had altruistic intentions. Even if they did something against another human being, I thought they were merely masking what the real hurt was on the inside. This may still be the case, however through many years of studying relationships, I have discovered there are people who outwardly seem altruistic but inwardly crave power, control, and recognition at the expense of others. This makes it very hard to know who to trust.

There are two old proverbs that I choose to live by (among others), "Choose a good name over great riches" (Prov. 22:1), and "Bad company corrupts good character" (1 Cor. 15:33). In other words,

1. People are not always what they seem.

2. Be careful who you affiliate yourself with.

If people are not always what they seem, then how do you develop trust in a relationship? We had better figure it out because one of the key building blocks of a healthy relationship is *trust*. Without it, there can be no authentic relationship.

BEGIN WITH TRUSTWORTHINESS

Have you ever had someone say to you, "Do you trust me?" Your answer to this question may be in the form of another question,

"To do what?"

Instead of blindly saying, "Yes, of course, I trust you," we would do well not to answer their question without first understanding the focus of it.

Trust is tricky. We try to generalize it, but in reality, it is complex and multi-faceted. It is often misunderstood even by many intelligent individuals. Onora O'Neill, an English philosopher, postures that when we say we need more trust, it is a "stupid aim," and that we should not be focused on building more trust, but rather trusting those who are trustworthy more and those who are untrustworthy less.[19]

I like this! Would we even need to ask the question "Do you trust me?" if we simply proved we were trustworthy by our actions and our words? So often we expect others to trust us without proving we are trustworthy first. We expect others to give us their trust just because we ask for it. However, trust comes as the result of trustworthiness. So if we want people to trust us more, how can we prove our trustworthiness? O'Neill believes trustworthiness must include these three components.

1. **Honesty**

   I used to tell my daughters while they were growing up (I still do, actually) that lying is wrong because it has the power to destroy a relationship very quickly. Lying and being caught in a lie is like napalm—it can flare up and burn out a relationship, charring it beyond repair. Honesty is a vital part of trustworthiness.

   A key component to honesty is accountability. Accountability is not a lack of trust; it is a test of honesty. Many times, it is wise to get a second opinion to confirm or verify the information given. Why else would you go get a second opinion from another doctor? Or on your car for a particular repair? Why would you talk to another friend regarding a situation you are facing after you just asked advice from the first one? Because a test of honesty that proves to be true deepens trust.

   I remember very distinctly when my wife was pregnant with our youngest daughter. The OB/GYN we had been with for eight months suggested Tania may have to get a C-section due to the size of our baby's head. Even though we trusted our doctor up to this point, this was not an acceptable option. We went to see another OB/GYN for a second opinion. The other OB/GYN evaluated Tania and our baby and concluded the baby's head was around nine cm, and although it may be a difficult delivery, it was not mandatory to have a C-section because the baby was not in any danger. This, of course, helped us (mainly Tania) feel more at ease. We went back feeling confident that the first doctor was looking out for the interests of Tania and the baby, but we decided to move forward without the C-section. We trusted the doctor to take us safely through the birth.

2. Competency

Competency literally means you have demonstrated skills and abilities in a particular area. I trust my ophthalmologist to treat issues and illnesses of my eyes, but I would not trust him with handling issues I have with my knees.

You wouldn't trust a ten-year-old to drive your car. They aren't competent to do so. You wouldn't trust someone you just met to housesit unless you did a background check and had them sign a form stating they are 100% responsible for all of your belongings while you are away (of course, that's not trust at all, is it?).

You wouldn't trust your dog alone with your fried chicken dinner, and you certainly wouldn't trust your mechanic to fly a jetliner on your trip to another country. However, you would trust that your dog will always come to you and be excited every time you walk into your home. You would trust your mechanic to bring your car back into operational status.

When you give trust to someone in some particular area of expertise, usually it is because they have proven they are willing and able to fulfill a specific task, assignment, or need. This speaks to competence.

3. Reliability

Dependable, devoted, faithful, truthful, and loyal. These are all words that describe someone who is reliable. There are people in your life who are competent at a specific skill, are honest in their words, but they may not be all that reliable.

When you give a time, and a place for someone to meet you and they don't show up, you are more likely going to have difficulty trusting that same person when you give them another place and time to meet. One miss does not mean they are unreliable. But two misses and one begins to doubt. Three misses, and your trust that the other person will ever be there on time wanes. This refers to reliability.

Trust is a must when trying to build a relationship with someone, whether it is a work relationship, friendship, romantic relationship, or a family relationship. But to develop trust between you and someone else, you need to prove you are trustworthy before you can be trusted. You would not expect anything less from someone else for you to trust him or her.

Perhaps trust is so difficult to give, and trustworthiness is so difficult to determine because many counterfeits are vying for our attention, money, time, and talents. To what end are the objects of our trust trying to obtain? Does the person or group we are placing our trust in have our best interests at heart? For that matter, do we have the best interests of others in mind?

There are thousands of attorneys in this country. Lawsuits are literally filling up dockets all across the nation. Why are we such a litigious society? Could it be that we have given up on proving the trustworthiness of others because it is so difficult to determine?

I used to give trust more readily than I do now. Skepticism is one of the results of broken trust throughout the years. I look more toward a person's trustworthiness before I give trust. Unfortunately, it is possible to sway more toward the skeptical side of thinking when you get burned too many times.

When building relationships with others, I am now trying to focus more on proving my own trustworthiness before expecting others to trust me. It doesn't mean I automatically trust others. In the process of establishing my own trustworthiness, I am surprised at how someone's true colors become known and reveal whether they are trustworthy or not.

Every time we walk into a new situation, a new job, or a new set of relationships, we begin the process of proving trustworthiness all over again. I used to get so tweaked at one particular job because I had to prove myself all over again. People questioned me, and I had to give an answer to my decisions, thoughts, and processes. Over time, I realized this is a natural part of life and necessary for any new relationship. We cannot expect someone to immediately trust us merely because we have a history of success in a certain area. It may take less time to get to that level of trust, but every new relationship or situation we walk into requires that we prove to be trustworthy.

Trust depends on the other person giving it to us. Trustworthiness doesn't depend on others; it depends on us. What would it look like if we lived in such a way with each other where we proved our own mettle before expecting to be given their trust? Would we even need so many levels of accountability, which are really only in place because of those who have proven to be untrustworthy?

Also, when we take the perspective that we need to prove our own trustworthiness before trust can be exchanged, maybe we would even be accepted by others sooner than later. Proving trustworthiness does take time, but it is an extremely valuable part of relationship—one worthy of mastering.

Repairing Broken Trust

Even though trust must be present to have a healthy relationship, we must realize at times that even those close to us will break trust on occasion. It will happen because we are humans living in a fallen world; all of us need God's grace and mercy in our lives.

We have all experienced the hurt of someone who broke trust in our relationship with them. Perhaps it was a child that lied, a co-worker that gossiped about something private you told them, a spouse who was unfaithful, or a pastor who had a moral failing. Maybe a close friend disappointed you in some way, or a politician broke a promise he or she made. Really, it could be anything anyone did that is the opposite of what they said or what you believed would happen.

Broken trust is difficult to mend, but it is possible. I have seen marriages come back from unfaithfulness, children come back into a trusting relationship with their parents, and employees come back and gain the good graces of their bosses.

How do we respond when trust is broken? What do we do? How about if we were the one who broke trust with someone? What do we do to rebuild it? There are two essential attitudes to embrace:

1. Vulnerability

   When trust is broken, a gap is created between the two people, and we tend to fill that gap with negative thoughts, beliefs, and a deeper lack of trust. The only way to bridge that gap requires a level of vulnerability on both sides. If you show a level of vulnerability, it has a positive effect on your ability to prove trustworthy to the other person.[20]

   If someone breaks your trust and they are significant to you, you may need to allow them to reestablish trust, which means taking the risk of them breaking it again. The one who is rebuilding the trust after it is broken needs to be vulnerable and allow the other person to hold them accountable by opening up their actions and thoughts to be tested. This process can take a long time, but it's important to remember that it is possible.

Trust can be restored. Relationships can be reconciled when we embrace vulnerability.

2. **Treat others as we want to be treated (Matt. 7:12).**

When we are considerate of others and their failings, we understand that we, too, are one decision or action away from breaking trust with someone. How would we want to be treated if we failed someone? We would want them to show us mercy, and we would want them to withhold judgment. The Scriptures tell us:

> "We who are strong must be considerate of those who are sensitive about things like this. We must not just please ourselves. We should help others do what is right and build them up in the Lord." (Rom. 15:1–2)

> "…because judgment without mercy will be shown to anyone who has not been merciful. Mercy triumphs over judgment." (James 2:13)

> "Why do you look at the speck of sawdust in your brother's eye and pay no attention to the plank in your own eye? How can you say to your brother, 'Let me take the speck out of your eye,' when all the time there is a plank in your own eye? You hypocrite, first take the plank out of your own eye, and then you will see clearly to remove the speck from your brother's eye." (Matt. 7:3–5)

We can be merciful and lead others to become more trustworthy, and we can work on our own trustworthiness. We can have more grace toward others when they fail us, and we can show mercy because we have been shown mercy. This will help repair broken trust.

TRUST REQUIRES RISK

Without trust, we cannot maintain deep relationships with others. It is a thread through all we do. In an article in *Psychology Today,* Peg Streep says the following:

> Trust is the foundation of all human connections, from chance encounters to friendships and intimate relationships. It governs all the interactions we have with each other. No one would drive a car or walk down a sidewalk, or board a train or an

airplane if we didn't "trust" that other people took their responsibilities seriously, and would obey whatever rules applied to
the endeavor at hand. We trust that other drivers will stay in
their lanes, that conductors and pilots will be sober and alert.
And that people will generally do their best to discharge their
obligations toward us. Culture, civilization, and community all
depend on such trust.[21]

A lack of trust leads to paranoia on our part. This concept has been written
about in business articles and books and has been dealt with in counseling
sessions all across this country. If we are going to take a step beyond acquaintance to friend, the gap of mistrust must be bridged between two people. This
applies in all of life—from family to friends to nations of the world.

But trust requires that we take certain risks. For example, when you sit
down on a chair, there is always a risk the chair has a flaw and will not be able
to hold you. There is a reason why business coaches and motivational speakers
will use the trust-fall exercise. When you stand with your back facing someone,
and you begin to fall backward, there is a risk that your partner won't catch
you. When the child jumps off the stairs or the edge of the pool, he trusts his
parent will be there to catch him. He is risking his own safety at times.

Some people would never walk out of their house, because they don't want
to risk sickness, hurt, pain, discomfort, or anything that would adversely affect
them. Fear can and will cripple us. Fear has a way of working its way into our
relationships—from past hurts, past betrayals, broken trust, and many other
relational issues and conflicts.

When a marital trust is broken, the fear becomes the idea that the person
we are married to can never be trusted again. The fear can also become the
thinking that anyone I may get close to will break that trust again. We can then
choose never to trust anyone fully again.

The risk, then, comes in taking the step, the leap, to trust others in relationship. However, may I suggest that trust in a relationship works best when in a
relationship with God first? When we love and trust God first, all of our other
relationships can be placed into perspective. When we love others as we love
ourselves, we prove trustworthy, and trust in our relationships becomes more
transparent.

We also have to be very aware of the standards and expectations we put
on people. Trust requires that our standards are reasonable and our expectations are fair. Standards become those non-negotiables in our lives that form the
basis for how we live and what we desire others to meet to have a relationship
with us. For example, being truthful even when difficult can be a standard we

set. Faithfulness can and should be a standard in our relationships.

The trouble comes when the standards become our expectations of others. If "not lying" is a standard, our expectation can be that someone will *never* lie to us. Since no one is perfect and all of us are one bad decision away from making a wrong choice, we will not be able to build trust with others, especially since we cannot even meet our own expectations in relationships with others all of the time. This is why forgiveness is so necessary.

We build trust with others when someone wrongs us and comes to us and asks for forgiveness. The standard would be if someone were to hurt us in some way, they would own it and come to us to reconcile. The expectation would be that they would *never* wrong us. Forgiveness and reconciliation should also become the standard because all of us fail.

We should not make our expectations the standards in our relationships. If we do, we set our relationships up for failure from the beginning. Standards are necessary. Expectations are our desires. The space between the two is where we exercise forgiveness, acceptance, understanding, and humility.

GOD IS TRUSTWORTHY

Jesus has more than earned our trust. He is the only One that has ever lived a sinless life. He proved his commitment to us by taking on the sin of the world—our sin—and loved us even before we had proven ourselves as trustworthy.

The Scriptures talk of trust and warn us not to place our *eternal* trust in *anyone* other than God Himself. Jeremiah 17:5–8 says,

> "This is what the Lord says, 'Cursed are those who put their trust in mere humans, who rely on human strength and turn their hearts away from the Lord. They are like stunted shrubs in the desert, with no hope for the future. They will live in barren wilderness in an uninhabited salty land. But blessed are those who trust in the Lord and have made the Lord their hope and confidence. They are like trees planted along a riverbank, with roots that reach deep into the water. Such trees are not bothered by the heat or worried by long months of drought. Their leaves stay green, and they never stop producing fruit.'"

Let the words of this passage sink into the deepest parts of your soul. When we trust in our finances to provide what we need, we will never have enough. When we trust our friends for our fulfillment, we will always come up short of feeling fulfilled. When we trust in a leader for complete guidance, we will not reach our full potential.

However, when we trust in God, we have everything we need—fulfillment, a pathway to reach our potential, and even more than all that—a hope that eternity is just around the corner of time. God will complete what He promised. We know this because He is trustworthy. Our trust in Him without having seen is called faith (Heb. 11:1).

Peter and Paul understood that we are going to struggle with trust in relationships. We are going to struggle with thinking of ourselves first and others second. But they give us a solution to this problem in Ephesians and 1 Peter:

> "Always be humble and gentle. Be patient with each other, making allowance for each other's faults because of your love. Make every effort to keep yourselves united in the Spirit, binding yourselves together with peace." (Eph. 4:2–3)

> "So humble yourselves under the mighty power of God, and at the right time he will lift you up in honor. Give all your worries and cares to God, for he cares about you." (1 Pet. 5:6–7)

Humility, patience, mercy, and unity must all be present in healthy relationships.

When we trust God first, He gives us the ability, through our humility before Him, to live in peace with others because we understand we all have faults. Trust can be built especially when both parties are trying to prove their own trustworthiness instead of expecting the other to do so first. Isaiah 26:3–4 promises, "You will keep in perfect peace all who trust in you, all whose thoughts are fixed on you! Trust in the Lord always, for the Lord God is the eternal Rock." A Scripture that many of us quote, yet use as a last resort sometimes says, "Trust in the Lord with all your heart; do not depend on your own understanding. Seek his will in all you do, and he will show you which path to take" (Prov. 3:5–6).

In relationships, trust is earned by proving our own trustworthiness. First and foremost, God gained our confidence even though He had nothing to prove by loving us before we knew or loved Him. Jesus died for us and demonstrated his trustworthiness. In a relationship, we can prove our trustworthiness because of him. By humbling ourselves, we can live in healthy relationships with others, building trust because of the fruit we produce in living according to his Word.

22.

The Art of Honesty

"The real things haven't changed. It is still best to be honest and truthful; to make the most of what we have; to be happy with simple pleasures; and have courage when things go wrong."
~ Laura Ingalls Wilder

"To believe in something, and not to live it, is dishonest."
~ Mahatma Gandhi

There were several weeks in 2015 when I had little to no motivation to write about relationships. Watching the fallout of the racial tension from Ferguson, the evil activities of terrorists in the Middle East, and my own battle with my identity had almost erased my desire to encourage people toward better and meaningful relationships. Then I was reminded of the importance that one voice might have in a dark world of preconceived notions, ignorance, and prevalent deception. I can choose to influence others with the truth about relationships. It is difficult. It is downright messy at times, but the reward of even just one changed relationship is worth it. One voice *can* have an impact.

It occurred to me that one of the most significant deterrents to healthy, meaningful relationships is deception and lying. We believe what is being presented to us (without testing), and we hide the truth because we are afraid of what others may think about us. Deception is one of God's primary concerns because He knows it separates us in the relationship with Him and each other.

Recently, I was reading about how early we as humans learn the skill of deception.[22] It was pointed out that as young as six months old, a child will come to understand that if she cries, someone will come and give her attention. At first, the cries are signals for food, a wet diaper, or affection. Then, like Pavlov's dog and the bell that became the stimulus for action, the parent responds out of routine, and the child now has her parents wrapped around her finger. At that point, the battle begins for who can outsmart the other. Will the parents recognize the deceptive attempts and respond, or will they teach the child the importance of crying only in the right circumstances?

At a certain point, children will even start to act like they are not doing something wrong when in fact they are well aware of their behavior. Setting their skill in motion, the child goes toward the cookie and picks it up to eat it. When the parent pops their head around the corner and catches them in the act, the response from the parent is, "No. Not before dinner." But the response from the child is to act like they are just looking at the cookie, and then gently place it back on the plate of cookie awesomeness. Children learn the art of deception early on.

How about the married relationship? What drives either person in this bond to lie? Perhaps it is to avoid an uncomfortable conversation or conflict. Truth be told (pun intended), if the deceptive behavior continues, it is only a matter of time before the foundation of the relationship crumbles and trust is all but lost. This is true for *all* relationships.

Have you ever heard someone say?

"Honestly…"

"To tell you the truth…"

"I cannot tell a lie…"

Why is it necessary to preface the truth with verification of its validity? I am more inclined to think that anyone who uses these expressions is lying most of the time, but this one fact that spills off their tongue *might* be the truth.

Honesty is not a scary venture if you never do anything to place yourself in the position of hurting someone, like an action you took or a conversation you had with another that broke a confidence. We feel the need to be deceptive whenever we are fearful of how that person will respond because we may have done something that causes them to be hurt *or* we have information that does damage.

For most people, lying is the preferred method of communication. It has become so ordinary that it can be quite challenging to determine which is the true statement. There are even games where you have to lie and hope that someone does not catch you in your lie. In a blog article from *The Huffington Post* called "Sixty Percent of Your Colleagues Are Lying to You," Dr. Travis Bradberry wrote, "University of Massachusetts psychologist Robert Feldman has studied lying for more than a decade, and his research has reached some startling conclusions. Most shocking is that 60% of people lie during a typical

10-minute conversation and they average two to three lies during that short timeframe." Dr. Bradberry goes on to report, "Most of the people in Feldman's studies don't even realize all of the lies they had told until after the conversation when it was played back to them on video."[23]

I don't know about you, but that is disturbing. No wonder we have such trouble with relationships. Some of us believe it is okay to lie sometimes, like lies that are meant to protect another's feelings. Make no mistake; lying has lasting effects. Any lie of any degree causes harm, both little white lies and big honking lies. The fact is any lie is an attempt to deceive. From what we discover in the Bible, God despises lies.

> "There are six things the Lord hates, seven things he detests: haughty eyes, a lying tongue, hands that kill the innocent, a heart that plots evil, feet that race to do wrong, a false witness who pours out lies, a person who sows discord in a family." (Prov. 6:16–19)

Notice that two of the top seven things God despises are about lying! When the Bible tells us these things, it is not meant to be another rule we have to follow just for the sake of the rule. All of the Ten Commandments, and all of what Jesus tells us in Matthew 22:37–39 has to do with two kinds of relationships: the one with him, and the one we have with each other. And one of the Ten Commandments refers specifically to lying in how we relate to one another, "You shall not bear false testimony against your neighbor" (Exod. 20:16). This literally means we shall not lie about what our neighbor did or did not do, said or did not say.

Why does God have such a harsh stance against deception and lying? Because they are relationship killers. Honesty may separate, but if you need to lie to maintain a relationship, chances are there is no authentic relationship there at all. Even that is deception.

Imagine your world without lying and deception. What if it were impossible to lie? Well, for one, there would be no need for judges. And policemen would have a much less difficult time interrogating the perpetrator of a crime. Married relationships would be more open. People might even be less inclined to do something wrong if they knew they *have* to tell the truth.

Kids would not be able to get away with anything, and parents would know exactly what their kids were doing when asked where they are. Relationships would be *way* more authentic, and we would know beyond a doubt who we could be in a relationship with. We could tell all others exactly what we think, and it would be okay.

In relationship, it is vitally important to be honest, forthright, truthful, and candid. But this seems to be a rarity nowadays and should be looked at. Lies slowly chip away at a relationship until there is nothing left that remotely resembles one. When someone is caught in a lie, whatever trust was there is eradicated by one phrase from the tongue.

I always taught my daughters while they were growing up that there are two things their mom and I would never tolerate in the home:

lying, and
disrespecting another individual

The reason we cannot tolerate those behaviors is that they are both self-serving and either one can destroy the relationship between two people. Ask yourself if it is worth killing the trust between you and a close friend or family member over one act of defiance, lack of trust, or desire to avoid a messy confrontation? Chances are if your relationship cannot withstand an error by either party, then the relationship was not built on the solid ground of truth and authenticity in the first place.

Take a day and perform an experiment. Go through your day and become aware of who you are talking to and what you are saying. Take inventory of your words and conversations, and notice when you tell a lie or try to deceive someone into thinking a certain way. I would bet that you will be *surprised* at how many times you catch yourself being dishonest. By-the-way, you cannot simply tag on the phrase "just kidding" after you do so. Sooner or later others will see through the ruse, and your true colors will come to the surface.

Dishonesty adds a heavy burden to our relationships. When we lie, we have to remember who we said what to keep our story straight; otherwise we are exposed. We can then start to believe the lie ourselves. Honesty relieves that burden.

Every day we should work toward honesty. Your relationships will become less of a struggle when you just tell the truth. Of course, the truth you tell must be mixed with love. If it is not combined with love, you endanger the relationship, and people will be less inclined to be your friend.

COMMIT TO HONESTY

If we are people who genuinely desire healthy, lasting relationships, then we must commit to the art of honesty. So where do we start? The easy answer is *"do not lie."*

Enough said.

Actually, I wish it were that easy. If being honest and truthful was easy, then we would not deceive each other so easily and freely.

"Deceive is such a strong word though. Telling a little white lie isn't the same as deceiving is it?"

Deception is lying and lying is deception. Both intend not to tell the truth. Dishonesty says something about our character. When we live dishonestly, we focus only on our own needs and wants and not the wants and needs of others— the very opposite of loving one another as yourself.

Take the proverbial question from the wife who asks, *"Honey, how do I look in this outfit?"* This simple question is one that puts a man in a difficult place for certain. However, if he doesn't like the outfit on her, how can he tell her honestly without hurting her feelings? The truth is the only reason he may lie to her would be self-seeking. He may try to justify the lie that he is "protecting her emotions," but what he is really doing is protecting himself from a bad night, the cold shoulder, or just wanting to leave the house because they are late for their dinner reservation.

Since we want to commit to honesty, though let's try this again.

Woman: *"Honey, how do I look in this outfit?"*

Man: *"Actually, it is not my favorite. I really like you in this other outfit. Would you consider wearing it?"*

That answer may still hold up your plans, but she will at least know you care and are listening to her. The next time she asks you, she knows you will be honest with her. I realize this is a silly example of a very serious situation.

When someone hears the word *honesty*, they may immediately think—harsh truth, hurtful, a reminder of our faults, etc. However, honesty delivered in love is what builds the trust in the relationship. Love and truth *must* be presented with honesty if a relationship is built on trust.

Keep in mind that being honest doesn't even mean the truth being told is going to come out the way you desire. The truth can come from someone in a variety of moods. However, if you know that person loves you and has your best interests at heart, even the harsh truth is better than allowing you to stumble and fall.

It takes time to build a relationship that has truth, honesty, and love as the foundation. Once it is built, lies and deception can make it come crashing down much faster than you can imagine. It does not mean you cannot build it again. Even if a house falls from the flames of deception, the debris that is left can be cleared, the foundation can be prepped again, and you can rebuild in the same spot.

Honesty and openness can be built in a relationship. What makes it that much stronger is accountability, the openness part. Committing to honesty also requires confession.

Confession Is Critical

> "But if we confess our sins to him, he is faithful and just to forgive us our sins and to cleanse us from all wickedness." (1 John 1:9)

> "Confess your sins to each other and pray for each other so that you may be healed. The earnest prayer of a righteous person has great power and produces wonderful results." (Jas. 5:16)

Rebuilding a relationship begins with confession. If I am the deceiver, I first need to confess my sins and the lies I told to God (1 John 1:9). He already knows they are not true. He just wants me to acknowledge that fact. When I present my faults to Him and ask Him for strength to tell the truth, it helps me to keep my focus on bolstering the relationship and not setting it up for failure through deception.

Next, I need to confess to the one I wronged. My goal here is to acknowledge my weakness and lovingly tell the truth. Confessing to one another helps to foster healing in our spirit and emotions, and it allows for openness in the relationship. It should end by praying together to ask God to mend the relationship and to avoid any future dishonesty or deception. Through prayer for each other, we will see amazing results in our relationships (Jas. 5:16).

If you'll remember something we learned in chapter 20,

> The "Principle of Structural Integrity"—that is, the ability to hold something together under its own weight and whatever load is placed in or on it. Instead of spaghetti, tape, and string though, we use trust, vulnerability, love, hope, support, respect, honesty, forgiveness, gratitude, good communication, connection, purpose, authenticity, and a host of others things as the relational building blocks for long-lasting relationships.

> These lifetime relationships are the kind that the Great Architect, God Himself, intends for us to have. His purpose in creating us is to be in a relationship with us and us with each other. If you desire a strong, structurally-sound relationship with anyone, it has to be built using these characteristics so that it can hold together and withstand whatever load is placed upon it, whether externally or emotionally.

Confession becomes the weight you place on the structure. And the relationship is as only as strong as the structure it is built upon. The good news about a relationship with God is that he already built the structure that can withstand any confession we have. Through Jesus and his death on the cross and overcoming all of that by rising from the dead, any and all sin that we confess to him and ask him to forgive us for can be erased. There is no confession he cannot handle (Ps. 103:12).

But for relationships with each other, some confessions can put too much weight on a relationship, depending on how stable their relational structure is. When first building a relationship, confession needs to start small. Letting someone know about your weaknesses is great, but you do not want to unleash your burdens too soon or all at once. As the structure of your relationship begins to strengthen, you can start to open up and confess more.

As you grow in relationship with others, you can begin to confess to others your weaknesses, but keep in mind that others will desire to do the same with you. It is the bond between *two* people that gives the relationship its strength. If only one person in that relationship is piling on the weight, it is sure to fail eventually. Some boundaries may need to be put in place if it gets to be too overwhelming.

Is True Honesty Possible?

This depends on the individual and the relationship. I believe it is possible, but it takes time, relational investment, working through difficulties, living within mutual boundaries with another, trust, and, most of all, an understanding of who we are—imperfect beings serving a perfect God.

One Saturday while teaching in a spiritual-life-training weekend, I utilized an illustration that I never expected to have the impact it did. The idea dropped into my mind a few weeks before the weekend while watching one of those cop shows. There was a one-way mirror they used to select the perpetrator, but the line-up couldn't see who was watching them through the mirror.

I hopped online and purchased a small one-way mirror; it measured about sixteen inches high, twelve inches wide, and about fourteen inches deep. When it came, I created this little box, purchased a light with a switch on the cord, and secured a picture of Jesus in the box on the wall opposite the one-way mirror.

Here is how the exercise went.

I set the box in the front of a room that seats about three hundred people. I positioned the box facing directly forward on a table behind me to my left as I faced the crowd, with a camera angled from the sound booth in the back of the room behind the crowd.

I set up the moment like this,

> This box represents us. When we look in the mirror, we see the reflection of who and what we are. We notice the flaws, the

mistakes, and the challenges we face. We cannot see inside this box, the box representing the heart as described in Scripture by Jeremiah,

> "The human heart is the most deceitful of all things, and desperately wicked. Who really knows how bad it is? But I, the Lord, search all hearts and examine secret motives. I give all people their due rewards, according to what their actions deserve." (Jer. 17:9–10)

Our hearts are dark, and even we cannot see how dark it really is. We can only reflect the outward appearance of who we believe we are to others. What makes up who we think we are can determine the course of any relationship positively or negatively.

We can pretend our faults don't exist and attempt to cover them up, but at the end of the day when we take off our masks, let our hair down, and settle into the privacy of our lives, we see reality staring back at us in the mirror. The reality is that our hearts are dark and even we do not understand our motives sometimes. We need to be honest with ourselves.

Something happens when we recognize our need for Jesus in our lives. When our eyes are opened, and we admit our sinful dark-hearted condition and accept the forgiveness Jesus gave to us through his death and resurrection, a *light* turns on in our heart! (Cue the light in the box.)

Everything that is dark in our hearts becomes exposed to the light as Jesus sets up residence in our lives. At the very moment when the light comes on, an image of Jesus automatically superimposes your own reflection in the mirror.

Now when you look at yourself in the mirror, you see Jesus *inside* you. You can now reflect a changed heart and a renewed mind to others because of the Light of Christ that resides in your heart. Others can now see Jesus *inside* of you, too. Because of Jesus, you can totally be honest with yourself and others, and you can live honestly with others.

When we live with the light of Jesus in our hearts, all of the dark places of our hearts are exposed. He makes them right by purifying our intentions and motives and allowing us to see ourselves and others through his eyes and perspective.

Honesty can become second nature in relationship because we know the Light of Christ will expose any false motive or deceptive idea. When he does, we can address honesty with great care, thereby protecting the relationships around us. I believe this leads to the kind of authentic, open, and healthy relationships God wants us to have.

23.

The Art of the Question

When I met Brian Griswold, he was the children's pastor where I had just become the Administrative Pastor in Maryland. At just about six foot two, he towered far above the little heads of children, and every single one of them absolutely loved him!

He served in children's ministry for almost thirty years. He has a boisterous laugh and an incredible sense of humor. He and his wife, Liz, created a family for themselves where mutual discussion and opinions were welcome. Why? Because they asked powerful questions.

Brian and I didn't become friends right away. We grew closer as we started to work together. By asking questions and listening to the responses, we became great friends where trust was easy, and our families coalesced. They brought such a different perspective into our lives, one that was new and refreshing!

I remember when Brian decided to leave the children's ministry and go into counseling and family therapy. He began to ask the question, "What if?" There is so much power in that question. In relationships, it is one of hope and excitement, but also can be one of dismay. For the most part, when asked, it can become a catalyst for stretching beyond our comfort zones and expanding our community of friends, experiences, and, therefore, enriching our lives even more.

It was when Brian left his position at the church that our friendship really began to take off. We met for lunch often to talk about our families, our children, the struggles we were facing, and the good things happening. Whenever I was experiencing specific struggles, Brian always asked me questions. These questions mined the motives of my heart, challenged me to think about the other's perspective, and always pointed me back to relationship over pride.

He never asked with condemnation, at least to my knowledge. I can remember chuckling on occasion because I knew what he was trying to do when he asked me questions, probing into my mind to pull out the intentions and feelings so he could get to the heart of the issue.

In turn, I began to ask him questions which he welcomed! This mutual friendship was deepened by the questions we asked each other because each of us proved trustworthy to the other. This then allowed me to open up to him about my past and the things in my life I had only shared with two or three people. He also opened up about the dark corners in his past. This was the confessing part I talked about in the previous chapter.

We should never underestimate the *power* of the question in relationship. Questions are so much better than assumptions or even statements. Making a statement into someone's life in relationship can hurt, be off-target, and cause damage. Asking questions, especially when said in context and with sincerity, have a way of opening up a relationship. It shows you are interested in the other person. It shows you have genuine concern for them, and you do not necessarily know the answer. It shows you are willing to walk through a life circumstance, discover, learn, and grow together.

Questions have a way of taking a shallow conversation into a deep-water dive where you can find answers you have always been looking for but could never see at the surface. As long as questions are present, relationships can continue to grow and develop. When questions cease in a relationship, it is only a matter of time before a separation begins to take place. We replace the questions with assumptions, implications, and doubt.

LISTENING

When Brian asked me a question, I didn't have to guess if he was listening to the answer. He actively leaned in and listened to my response, not rushing the answer, and allowed me to take my time to prep my thoughts to respond. When I needed clarification, he asked the question in a different way, knowing that we all receive and interpret messages uniquely.

By listening, he asked another question about something I had just said. This told me that not only was he listening, but he picked up something in my response that required more depth and thought. His listening showed his brother-like love for me.

This is the best way to get to know someone, to know who they are and how they think. Questions have a wonderful way of bringing clarity to a relationship, purpose to a conversation, and opportunities for trust to be confirmed. Listening intently and intentionally to the things said and unsaid will inevitably raise more questions. We can continue to be relational archaeologists, brushing away the dirt and debris to get to the "find." We uncover more of how someone ticks, what has brought them to where they are now, and even why they may act or respond in certain life situations.

THE QUEST FOR QUESTIONS

Questions are the doorbells to relationship; ask the right ones, and someone might let you in. In almost every aspect of life, questions are present. They are everywhere. For instance,

- When you go to a job interview, you will receive questions.
- When you are learning a new subject in school, you will be quizzed with questions.
- On any job application, you will need to answer questions.
- If you go to court, you will be asked questions.
- When you walk into a restaurant, you are faced with questions.
- When you meet someone new, you will answer questions.

Brian taught me so much about asking questions. When we offer an opinion on something without asking questions, we do not allow ourselves to gain more information, and we can easily misjudge and miscommunicate.

Whenever I first meet with someone, whether it is casual, ministry related, or the beginning of a coaching relationship, I have a list of questions I like to ask so I can get to know the person and their history. The very first questions I ask anyone I am sitting down with for the first time are:

"Where were you born?"
"How did you get to where you are right now?"

Usually, they are followed with a laugh, but with a straight face, I respond, "No, really. Tell me all you want about the time between your birth and where you are now. I may stop you during your story and ask more questions if that is okay?"

Most people settle in very quickly and begin their story. Inevitably, during the story, the person will make a statement such as, *"Then I moved from Baltimore to California,"* or, *"Then I went to the University of Colorado."* Making statements like these beg for another question. *"Why did you move from Baltimore to California?"* or, *"Why did you choose the University of Colorado?"* These insights let you see into a window of their choices. What someone does is not as important as *why* they choose it. Where someone goes is not as important as why they choose to go there. You're trying to get to the *why* behind things.

If you are actively listening, there are parts of a person's story that they leak out when they are telling their history. I'll give you an example from my own story.

> *"In 2006, my wife accepted an internship at the University of Maryland, and in January of 2007, she was accepted into the residency program there. Four months later, my kids and I moved out to Maryland with her."*

What jumps out at you in these comments? What kinds of questions come to mind when you reread it?

There is so much that can happen in a year, but there is one fact that jumps out at you. Other facts could lead to more in-depth questions, which I would ask permission to dive into.

The first question one might ask is this, *"When you say, 'the kids and I moved out to Maryland with her,' did the two of you live in different places that year?"*

Then other questions might follow, *"May I ask how you felt being so far away from your wife for one year? Did you see each other during that year? Did you both work and take care of the kids in that year?"*

You could also probe a little deeper and ask, *"What was the most difficult thing you faced as a single dad during that time frame? Why did you decide not to move when she accepted her internship? How did that time away from each other affect the relationship with your wife?"*

People usually leak out information and insight into their past that might raise the curiosity hairs on the back of your neck. When that happens, make sure you give them the freedom not to share something that is too personal at this early stage in the relationship.

Brian taught me, without even knowing it, that asking the right questions and giving someone the freedom to answer or not can build trust between people. It also shows there is interest in the other person.

Too often when we meet people for the first time, we expect they will want to hear about what we are doing now, where we work, where we live, how many kids we have, and so on. However, this information is only floating on top of the surface.

My philosophy, especially after my friendship with Brian, rests on the fact that I start off thinking this person may not want to hear about my life. If I treat people how I want to be treated, I will ask them about their life. Sometimes it opens the door to a relationship, and they return the questions. Sometimes it does not. That is a risk we take.

You have experienced it, and you have probably done it yourself: you ask someone you know, *"How are you doing?"* Their answer? *"Fine."*

Most people will not offer anything more than that response. Brian asked me more direct questions that made me think. Now when I am continuing to get to know someone, I ask questions like, *"What is the best thing that has happened to you this past week?"* Or, *"Is there something you are really looking forward to or planning in your life?"* I may follow up with, *"Is there something or someone in your life I can pray for that is weighing you down?"*

These questions leave room for the person to decide how much to share and what to share. It is more meaningful than just asking how they are doing. The questions are not threatening, and they help you to get to know someone as they open up and share the answers with you. Often, they will return the same question in response, so make sure you have thought it through!

When you ask permission to ask deep questions, the conversation is less like a jail cell and more like freedom on the open road. You can take any avenue off the main path to discover together—things about each other that will enhance your relationship with the other. Then, when people come to your mind, you will automatically know how to pray for them.

QUESTIONS AND CONFLICT

Quite often, even though we were created for relationship, sin and pride get between people. We hold our possessions in higher regard than our relationships sometimes. We often consider ourselves first which can be a hindrance to the relationship. We over-analyze someone else's behavior or words until we have embellished the story in our minds so much that it separates us in relationship.

Conflict sucks. Even though it may seem some people thrive in conflict and almost seek it out to survive, I believe most of us would rather not have to deal with the emotions or thoughts that come along with the conflict.

Questions can open the window so you can air out grievances and get a better understanding of the conflict, but not questions like these,

"Why are you such an idiot?"

"What is wrong with you!?"

"Why can't you understand your problem?"

For the obvious reason, these questions can be considered borderline verbal abuse. In any conflict, we would be wise to take a moment to settle our emotions and objectively think through what is going on before asking any questions. Then the questions we may wish to ask should help get to the heart of the issue, like the following,

> *"Okay, so this is what I heard or felt; is this what you meant?"*
>
> *"Would you help me understand..."* (fill in the blank with the issue)
>
> *"Is there something I said or did that may have caused you to be hurt or offended?"*

These questions are probing questions to help us process through a conflict, and if you are receptive to the answers, they can help to resolve the conflict and even draw you closer to the person you have the conflict with. Of course, you cannot guarantee this. However, you will know you did what was necessary to try and reconcile.

GET-TO-KNOW-YOU QUESTIONS

When I am trying to get to know someone, I begin by asking questions to uncover as much as I can through them sharing their story about what has made them into who they are today. But it cannot stop there. As I continue to spend more time with this person, I move on to "get-to-know-you" types of questions.

There are two specific questions I like to ask that probe a little deeper into how a person may think. It may sound silly, but I have found it says a lot about a person when you hear their answer, for better or for worse. If the situation ever presents itself and you have time to walk through the answers together, try these questions with someone you know well.

"What is your favorite reality TV show, and why?"

Listen very intently and try not to react in any way when they answer. It can be any number of reality TV shows. Remember, the *why* behind their answer is what you are looking for. After they respond, be ready to describe what yours is and why.

My favorite reality TV show is *America's Got Talent*. (Don't judge me!) The reason why I watch this show is to witness that moment—the moment someone gets up on the big stage with a few thousand people, four judges, and the potential of millions of TV watchers watching them... the room gets quiet, and the stage belongs to them. They perform their talent to the best of their ability. After they are done, the audience erupts into applause, the judges are standing on their feet, and those at home respond in kind. It's not until after the contestant is done that they realize what just happened.

Whatever struggle they faced to get to that stage; whatever nerves they had, wondering how the audience would respond; whatever negative comments they received by people who tried to hold them back; whatever issues they had—for just ninety seconds, all of it fell away, and they did what they loved to do. The audience, the judges, and we at home loved it.

That moment when they realize their performance and their talent is recognized and appreciated, and they well up with emotion—*that* is the reason why I love this show. Overcoming obstacles, negative feelings, negative people, negative situations in their lives, and being affirmed in their passion in life is well worth the time. I celebrate with them as they have already won the show.

Another favorite reality TV show I used to watch was *Extreme Home Makeover*. It was always the last ten minutes of the show when Ty Pennington would *"move that bus,"* and the family would see their new home for the first time. Their reactions of disbelief, celebration, crying, appreciation, and all the emotions that come with receiving something you feel you don't deserve come bursting through the television screen. I cannot help but laugh, cry, and celebrate with them. These moments when someone gets to experience a *win*, and we get to witness it—this is why I love those shows.

This is the same reason why I am a pastor. I live for the moment when someone realizes all their sins can be forgiven just because they have made a confession of faith in Jesus Christ and his sacrifice and resurrection. They just received a gift they could never buy and never earn, and they will never again be the same.

When someone's eyes and hearts are open to receiving the gift of eternal life with God, *that* moment is my favorite moment. A few others that come close are when an *A-ha!* moment happens because someone has just learned another nugget of information that will help them in their life and relationships. I love when reconciliation happens between two people, and I love being able to bless someone with something that makes their day and helps them to understand how God sees them and loves them. Those are the moments I live for.

The disciples had that kind of *A-ha!* moment with Jesus. Mark 8:27–30 describes a time when the disciples had been traveling with Jesus for some time. They had eaten with him, walked with him, witnessed him perform mind-blowing miracles—things they had never seen before—and they talked with and learned from him daily.

The disciples learned that a relationship with God involves questions. They asked questions all the time of Jesus! And Jesus was always asking them questions. It is not just us that asks questions of God; sometimes God asks questions of us.

The difference here is that since God already knows us inside and out, the questions He asks can be to test us, to see how far along we are in our growing faith walk, or even in response to one of our questions. We see Jesus doing this throughout his ministry on this earth.

One such time is recorded in Matthew 16:13–20. Jesus and his disciples had arrived in Caesarea Philippi, and while they were spending some time together, Jesus decided to ask them who others say that He is. The murmur of the crowds had entered their ears, and they responded by saying, "Some say John the Baptist, some say Elijah, and others say Jeremiah or one of the other prophets."

This was just a precursor question. Then Jesus asked them directly, "But who do you say I am?"

Peter chimed in and said, "You are the Messiah, the son of the Living God." There it was. Peter just made a declaration of faith right there. Because of the time he had spent with Jesus, he understood *who* Jesus is.

The question Jesus asked brought the disciples to the doorway of faith. If they made this confession of faith about who Jesus really is, they could walk through the door to a deeper relationship with Him.

Ask the right question and someone might let you in.

This is an example for us. How deep are you allowing your relationships to go? Questions are the shovels that help us dig deeper into relationship. Some may be afraid of what someone may uncover that has been buried for a long time. However, the more we expose ourselves to those we trust, the deeper we can go, and the more meaningful our relationships can be. Without probing questions, our relationships will only stay on the surface.

Never Stop Asking Questions

We should always be on the quest for discovery about people in our life. Even after twenty-plus years of marriage, there are still things I am learning about my wife. I still need to ask questions to learn what she may be thinking. It shows my love for her and lets her know I am interested in her life.

God, Himself is unfathomable and outside time; who could possibly know and understand all there is about God? No one! Asking questions is one of the best ways to continue to develop an understanding of God and move into a deeper relationship with Him. When we do ask Him questions, we should listen very carefully to the answers He gives, as they can be verbal or non-verbal.

Even though man is a created being, who could possibly know and understand all there is about someone? No one except God, of course. Asking questions is one of the best ways to continue to develop an understanding of others and move into a deeper relationship with them.

God has created us for relationship. There are always going to be new people that enter into my life that I can get to know. Questions help us on our journey to discover the lost art of relationship. It is one of the keys to developing into the kind of person who humbles themselves and does not think they are higher than others. If you don't ask questions, could it be that we think we are better than those around us and have it all figured out?

It always feels good to know the answer, and it starts with a question!

Why not go on a journey of discovery?

Are you ready?

Conclusion

Why should we connect with others?

By now, I'm hoping you know why!

It benefits me. It benefits you. It should benefit others. It pleases God.

I have seen so many relationships suffer due to pride, including some of mine due to my own pride. At the very core, pride rots our relationships and keeps us from developing meaningful connections with others.

We all have several things in common: all of us have had relationships fail; all of us have relationships we are struggling with even now; all of us need healthy relationships with others; all of us need a relationship with God.

No matter where we are in life, rediscovering the lost art of relationship can help us grow and develop meaningful connections with others, thereby enhancing our lives, building our businesses, expanding our personal communities, lifting our churches, encouraging others, and leaving us with no regrets at the end of our lives.

If you are a youth, remember to value others.

If you are a young adult, remind yourself you need others.

If you are a middle-aged adult, remember your purpose in relationships.

If you are a seasoned adult, remind yourself that you are still valuable—as long as you have breath in your lungs, you can be an influence in relationships.

Take the chance in your relationships. Ask questions. Lay aside your inhibitions. Become a servant. Be a friend. Prove yourself trustworthy. Be humble. Be honest. Build a strong foundation. Hold on to hope. Understand that influence is way better than authority. Don't allow jealousy to taint your relationships. Forgive. Pray. Give people a second chance. Treat others how you want to be treated. Build your community. Understand your purpose in relationship. And most of all, love others as you love yourself.

Like an archaeological dig, I hope you will begin to unearth the lost commandment "to love others as you love yourself." When you do, may you start to live a fulfilled, abundant life through your relationship with God and your relationships with others.

✤ Appendix 1 ✤

FOOT-WASHING SERVICE SCRIPT

The following is the script I read during a foot-washing service conducted between a group of pastors and the leadership team of Successful Christian Fellowship as referenced in chapter 11. I hope it inspires you to perform a foot-washing service of your own someday. It was profoundly significant and moving.

This was no small thing that Jesus was trying to show his disciples. He was teaching them that no one in the body of Christ is greater than Jesus himself. If Jesus could get down on his knees as a servant would and wash his disciple's feet, then surely, we can do the same for each other.

As a matter of fact, he even said to us, "Now that I, your Lord and Teacher, have washed your feet, you also should wash one another's feet. I have set you an example that you should do as I have done for you." (John 13:12–17)

There are two specific words I have in my heart that I believe have come from the Lord as a word of blessing over the leadership of Successful Christian Fellowship.

This example we are giving today is not to be taken as a trivial spectacle, but as a sincere, meaningful expression of our duty to each other as the body of Christ.

I don't have any clue how you will receive this today, those who are watching this. I do know that for those who are involved, it is a truly humbling experience. As a matter of fact, for those receiving it, you will probably feel like you should be the one washing. I am sure that you would do the same for us if the opportunity presented itself.

First, to the leadership of Successful Christian Fellowship: we want to communicate more than anything else to you our love for you as brothers and sisters in the Lord. We are part of the same family because of our faith in Jesus Christ through his death and resurrection, which we will remember and celebrate in a few short weeks.

Please remove your shoes and socks.

This first act of removing your shoes and socks is a symbol of our vulnerability before God. One of the parts of the body which we stay away from on most people is their feet. Your feet take the brunt of your travels. They are a representation of our lives as believers. Sometimes it stinks. Sometimes it is very tiresome. Sometimes it hurts.

Everyone, wash the feet of the one in front of you. First the right, then the left.

Everyone, now take the lotion provided to you and gently massage the lotion into the tops of the feet of the one in front of you. First the right, then the left.

The first thing I would like to speak to your lives and ministry is this:

> "You have been working hard for the Lord. You have remained faithful even when you felt like you could not take one more step. Be washed and refreshed right now through the washing of your feet. You are entering into a time of refreshing before the Lord. Be renewed."

The second thing I would like to speak to your lives and ministry is this:

> "This lotion is a symbol of the covering of the power of the Holy Spirit who brings rest, comfort, and peace. The Holy Spirit also gives the power to be witnesses. Now rise and let your feet be fitted with the readiness that comes from the gospel of peace."

Receive the blessing of the Lord over your lives and over your ministry.

⟨⊹⟩

⚜ Notes ⚜

(1) Gladwell, Malcom, 1963–. *Outliers: The Story of Success*. New York: Little Brown and Co., 2008. Print.

(2) Winerman, Lea. "'Thin slices' of life." *Apa.org*. http://www.apa.org/monitor/mar05/slices.aspx. Accessed August 20, 2016.

(3) Eliot, T.S., *Murder in the Cathedral*. New York: Faber and Faber, 1938. Print.

(4) "Forgiveness: Your Health Depends on it." *Hopkins Medicine*. 2015, https://www.hopkinsmedicine.org/health/healthy_aging/healthy_connections/forgiveness-your-health-depends-on-it.

(5) "Honor" Def. 13. Dictionary.com. August, 2018. Web. 17, June, 2017.

(6) "Honor" Def. 8. Merriam-webster.com. *Merriam-Webster Dictionary*, August, 2018. Web. 17, June, 2017.

(7) Chrystal, Dan. Foot-washing script in Appendix 1.

(8) Marshall, Michelle. "26 Powerful Quotes to Motivate You to Overcome Your Fears," www.thoughtcatalog.com. https://thoughtcatalog.com/michelle-marshall/2018/01/26-powerful-quotes-to-motivate-you-to-overcome-your-fears/. Accessed August 27, 2018.

(9) Cloud, Henry, and John S. Townsend. *Boundaries: When to Say Yes, When to Say No to Take Control of Your Life*. (Grand Rapids: Zondervan, 1992). Print.

(10) https://www.brainyquote.com/quotes/desmond_tutu_454129. Last accessed on August 27, 2018.

(11) Schuller, Robert H. Robert H Schuller Quotes. *Goodreads.com*. https://www.goodreads.com/quotes/522234-let-your-hopes-not-your-hurts-shape-your-future. Accessed June 21, 2017.

(12) Murray, Andrew, Humility. The Fig Classic Series, 2012. Electronic Edition.

(13) Barber, Trish. "60+ Ways to Use Salt." *Rd.com*. http://www.rd.com/home/cleaning-organizing/over-60-ways-to-use-salt/. Accessed April 15, 2017.

(14) Cartwright, Mark. "Corinth." *Ancient.eu/Corinth*. Posted on September 2, 2009. https://www.ancient.eu/corinth/. Accessed June 23, 2017.

(15) McBride, Louis. "How Immoral was the City of Corinth—Really?" *bbhchurchconnection.com*. Posted on January 9, 2015. https://bbhchurchconnection.wordpress.com/2015/01/09/how-immoral-was-corinth-really/. Accessed May 25, 2017.

(16) "Introduction to Structural Integrity." *open.edu*. http://www.open.edu/openlearn/ocw/mod/oucontent/view.php?id=3459&printable=1. Accessed January 3, 2017.

(17) Wujec, Tom. "Build a tower, build a team." *YouTube,* uploaded by TED.com. February 2010, https://www.ted.com/talks/tom_wujec_build_a_tower?language=en.

(18) "Prototype." Def. 1. *Merriam-webster.com*. Merriam-Webster Dictionary, Aug., 2018. Web. 12, June, 2017.

(19) O'Neill, Onora. "What we don't understand about trust." *YouTube,* uploaded by TED.com. 25 September 2013. https://www.youtube.com/watch?v=1PNX6M_dVsk.

(20) O'Neill, Onora. "What we don't understand about trust." *YouTube,* uploaded by TED.com. 25 September 2013. https://www.youtube.com/watch?v=1PNX6M_dVsk.

(21) Streep, Peg. (2014). "The Trouble with Trust." *PsychologyToday.com*. https://www.psychologytoday.com/blog/tech-support/201403/the-trouble-trust. Accessed April 15, 2017.

(22) Myer, Pamela. *LIESPOTTING: Proven Techniques to Detect Deception.* New York: St. Martin's Press, 2010. Digital Print.

(23) Bradberry, Dr. Travis. "Sixty Percent of Your Colleagues Are Lying to You," *The Huffington Post*. Posted on February 14, 2016. http://www.huffingtonpost.com/dr-travis-bradberry/sixty-percent-of-your-col_b_9044758.html. Accessed May 20, 2017.

✢ About the Author & The Sophos Group ✢

Dan Chrystal is an avid student of relationship. With over twenty-three years of ministry and relationship experience, Dan serves as one of the pastors at Bayside Church under the dynamic leadership of founding pastor, Ray Johnston. He is on Bayside's Thrive leadership team, a growing conference that reaches thousands of leaders every year, where he oversees sponsorship acquisition and curating church relationships.

Dan is a vibrant speaker and a dedicated life, career, and couple's coach. He is the owner of The Sophos Group, a coaching and consulting firm, and he also oversees the business side of his wife's corporation. He holds an MBA in executive leadership from Kaplan University (now Purdue Global University) and is currently studying law at Concord Law School.

His extensive ministry background has taken him all over the country, and he has served in varying capacities, including Lead Pastor, Administrative Pastor, Associate Pastor, Worship Leader, and Youth Pastor. He has lived in Baltimore, near Philadelphia, inner-city New Jersey, Central Coast California, Los Angeles, and now Northern California. In each place, Dan has developed deep and meaningful relationships with many people.

A champion for connecting people, relationships are at the core of who he is. It is not uncommon to find him spending time with others at coffee shops, restaurants, offices, or at his home getting to know as many people as his schedule allows.

His passion, mission, and purpose are to pass along what he has learned about relationship from key people in his life, helping others understand and put into practice what "loving their neighbors as themselves" truly means.

Dan and his wife, Tania, live in Lincoln, California. Together they have two daughters, two grandchildren, three dogs, and a full life! Connect with Dan through email at thesophosgroup@gmail.com.

"Choose a good reputation over great riches."
Proverbs 22:1

CPSIA information can be obtained
at www.ICGtesting.com
Printed in the USA
FSHW011533050319
56071FS

9 781732 756403